HARRY POTTER
A CHRISTIAN CHRONICLE

Sonia Falaschi-Ray

To Jeremy
with all good wishes.

Sonia F-R.

Book Guild Publishing
Sussex, England

First published in Great Britain in 2011 by
The Book Guild Ltd
Pavilion View
19 New Road
Brighton, BN1 1UF

Typeset in Garamond by
Ellipsis Digital Limited, Glasgow

Printed in Great Britain by
CPI Group (UK) Ltd, Croydon, CR0 4YY

A catalogue record for this book is available from The British Library.

ISBN 978 1 84624 681 4

**To the Glory of God: Father, Son and
Holy Spirit.**

*To my husband John, whose erudition and
encouragement are greatly appreciated, to my mother
Enid, for her unwavering support and to Quintus,
whose dogliness instructs me in the art of being.*

Contents

Foreword

Almost as soon as I heard about the first Harry Potter book, I heard about the critical responses of some Christian leaders. Members of some congregations were warned not to buy the book for fear of being drawn into the world of the occult. Others were encouraged to buy copies and burn them on bonfires. So I went out and bought *Harry Potter and the Philosopher's Stone* and read it for myself, thus beginning an enduring friendship with Harry, Hermione and Ron and the many other characters in the books, and placing myself with complete confidence into the hands of a consummate and trustworthy storyteller.

What I quickly discovered was, far from being a sinister and unsavoury book, one I would prevent my own children from reading, Harry Potter was an absorbing tale of the struggle between good and evil, with a boy hero who displayed a Christ-like response in the face of ignorance, hostility and abuse. I was amazed at J.K. Rowling's creative imagination and sheer cleverness, and, as a fellow writer, found myself wishing I had invented things like the Invisibility Cloak, paintings with subjects that move and speak and maps that show everyone's position. My only regret was that the books had not been written when I was ten or eleven years old, so that I could have grown up with the stories. I know I would have had a serious crush on Harry Potter! Coming to them as an adult was, however, still wonderful and on many train journeys in the late

1990s and into the new century, I would catch the eye of another grown up, who, like me, was deeply engrossed in one of the epic sagas.

As a Christian and a Harry Potter fan, I am so grateful to Sonia Falaschi-Ray for writing this book. Sonia brings remarkable insight to the Harry Potter books and offers a most helpful and perceptive analysis. She has delved deep into the stories and has shown that, far from being dangerous or subversive of Christianity, the books draw on much biblical material and uphold core Christian values.

In the first section of this book, 'Christian Characterisation', Sonia analyses a dozen of the main characters and points out similarities between them and certain biblical characters and principles. Her comparisons between the young Harry Potter and the Christ child are most intriguing, as is her suggestion that as Harry develops, he is presented with a number of similar challenges and temptations as those faced by Jesus.

Sonia's comments are also enhanced by her comparison to many other stories, from the great Greek and Roman myths to the Arthurian legends, and to other writers ranging from St John of the Cross to George Orwell. She draws helpfully and impressively on her knowledge of a number of other disciplines, notably philosophy and psychology. I found Sonia's comparison of attitudes towards the various wizard blood lines and racism to be particularly insightful, as is her discussion of the concept of the 'greater good'.

In the section on 'World View', Sonia identifies and catalogues many topics addressed in the books. Here, as in the section on the main characters, she provides brief but valuable analyses of these subjects, from views on gender equality to the perils of an unscrupulous and manipulated press. Also most helpful are Sonia's identification of some of the archetypal imagery that J.K. Rowling uses and a section on some of the biblical texts that refer to magic.

As Sonia shows, the Harry Potter stories are far from trite, predictable or facile and do not shrink from a whole host of painful subjects and universal themes, such as fear, betrayal, jealousy and death. In fact, J.K. Rowling takes her characters through some desperately heartrending and challenging experiences, where they are tested to the limit. Along the way, good people are hurt and killed and bad people wreck havoc, yet, in common with all good fairy stories, in the end, good triumphs over evil.

Perhaps it is more accurate to say that, in the end, love triumphs over evil, for it is love, and in particular, self-sacrificing love, that enables Harry Potter ultimately to vanquish his terrifying enemy. It was this love that prompted Harry's mother to protect him, thereby ensuring her own death, and it is this love that Harry eventually chooses in order to defeat Lord Voldemort, the personification of all that is craven and distorted in our natures, ruled by a bloodthirsty hatred and hunger for power.

If you are a veteran Harry Potter fan, this book will deepen and enlarge your appreciation of these remarkable stories and open your eyes to even more fascinating facts and insights. If you are new to the series, this book will give you a most helpful introduction to the complex characters and complicated plots, with an appreciation and analysis from a Christian perspective. As for me, it has inspired me to read the Harry Potter books all over again, starting from the beginning, this time with new insights and a deeper understanding.

Christina Rees
May 2011

Acknowledgements

Many thanks are due to Carol Biss, Jon Ingoldby and the rest of the team at the Book Guild for their support and speedy preparation of my script. I would also like to thank the following for all their help, advice and encouragement: Margaret Bowker, Matthew Cocksworth, Enid Falaschi, Sylvia Kinder, Carrie Pemberton, John Ray, Chris Rees, Christina Rees, Imogen Scowen, Maxine Scowen, Mike Thompson, Susanne Thompson, Diane Walker and Gareth Wardell.

Biblical quotes taken from the *New Revised Standard Version* (Zondervan Interactive The Zondervan Corp 1998, 5300 Patterson Avenue SE Grand Rapids, MI 49530 USA) and the original Greek text, unless otherwise stated.

Harry Potter books by J.K Rowling, Bloomsbury Publishing Plc, 36 Soho Square, London W1D 3QY

Harry Potter and the Philosopher's Stone Copyright © J. K. Rowling 1997

Harry Potter and the Chamber of Secrets Copyright © J. K. Rowling 1998

Harry Potter and the Prisoner of Azkaban Copyright © J. K. Rowling 1999

Harry Potter and the Goblet of Fire Copyright © J. K. Rowling 2000

Introduction

Are the Harry Potter books compatible with Christian teaching? Should they be shunned because they contain witchcraft? Which Christian characters, values and situation parallels are explored in them? How could they be used for biblical teaching? If you are concerned about or interested in these issues, this book is for you.

I am troubled that some Christians have condemned the Harry Potter series and have influenced others who, were they to read the books or see the films, would realise that, far from being anti-Christian, they contain the core Christian message, much orthodoxy, symbolism and many of Jesus' moral precepts. They are also grippingly entertaining stories tapping into our rich heritage of myth, legend and fantasy. They demonstrate J. K. Rowling's fertile imagination and keen sense of humour, as well as her profound understanding of psychology and the human condition. The fear that Harry Potter might lead children into the occult I believe to be without foundation.

Firstly I analyse some of the characters in Harry Potter and their parallels with biblical persons and experiences – for example, Harry himself is a Christ-like figure. He has a troubled infancy, surviving a murder attempt. He has unusual powers, is uncorrupted by temptations and witnesses to the truth. His destiny is to overcome evil by offering up his life. Rubeus Hagrid is the huge Hogwarts School gamekeeper. He displays many character traits of Jesus' disciple Simon Peter. Hagrid is honest, loyal, impulsive, prone to indiscretion and fearsomely strong. His heart is in the right place but he frequently puts his foot in his mouth. Professor Severus Snape is, arguably, the most complex character in the books. He has a Pauline–like conversion from serving evil to serving the cause of goodness. However, he dissembles, 'being all things to all men that some might be saved'.

Secondly I examine Rowling's world view. For example, authority, its source and its potential to be corrupted, also racism, gender equality, slavery, holiness of life and the need for remorse, repentance, to turn from serving evil to serving good. I compare and contrast Harry Potter and Christian approaches to death, bereavement and the afterlife. I also address Rowling's use of Christian imagery and symbolism and the power of love. I explore in context what the Bible says about witchcraft and why these books are unlikely to draw children into it.

Thirdly I have included a study guide. This takes issues raised and, using examples from Harry Potter, the Old and the New Testaments, invites readers to examine how they might be relevant now, and how they might handle such predicaments in the light of what they have read.

J.K. Rowling was brought up an Anglican and is now a member of the Church of Scotland. In an interview launching *Harry Potter and the Deathly Hallows*, she said, 'To me, the religious parallels have always been obvious . . . but I never wanted to talk too openly about it because I thought it might show people who just wanted the story, where we were going . . . I think those two particular [biblical] quotations he [Harry] finds on the tombstones, they sum up, they almost epitomise, the whole series.'[1] These are, 'Where your treasure is, there will your heart be also' and 'The last enemy that shall be destroyed is death'.[2]

1

Christian Characterisation

Harry Potter is not a straightforward Christian allegory, as none of the characters is an exact representation of any biblical person. However, many of them display distinctive characteristics of such people. Moreover, many of the themes and indeed the general ethical thrust of the books are clearly of a Christian nature. The characters also display features found in Egyptian, Classical and Nordic mythology, not to mention fairy tales.

Harry Potter

Harry Potter can be compared with the Christ child and also with mythic and comic-book superheroes. His infancy is fraught with difficulties; his parents were both wizards, but his mother, Lily, was born to 'Muggle' (i.e. non-magical) parents. The problems this caused her and her family, as she grew up in a conventional household whilst attending Hogwarts School of Witchcraft and Wizardry, left a legacy of resentment in her 'normal' sister Petunia. Petunia finds herself bringing Harry Potter up from the age of one, after his parents are killed in an attempt to assassinate him. Superheroes from Hercules, son of the ancient Greek god Zeus and mortal Alcmene, to Superman from the planet Krypton, adopted and raised by humans, had similar parental problems.

There were even rumours that Alexander the Great was not the son of King Philip of Macedon but that his mother had an unhealthy relationship with snakes. Then we can think of Jesus, whose mother Mary was impregnated by God the Holy Spirit. Joseph, Mary's fiancé, wanted to break off his engagement on finding Mary pregnant until informed in a dream that God was the boy's father and that they should call him Jesus (the Greek form of Joshua, meaning 'the Lord saves'), as he would save people from their sins. The infant Jesus survived Herod's murder attempt. In C.S. Lewis' book, *The Lion the Witch and the Wardrobe*, the lion Aslan is presented as an obviously allegorical Christ figure, due to his being prepared to suffer and die for the benefit of his magical world. He is subsequently resurrected. Conservative Christians who decry the Harry Potter books seem to revere the *Narnia* chronicles, irrespective of their magic and mythical setting. Harry Potter of course behaves similarly, being prepared to die as the one way to defeat the power of evil. However, the initial Christian outcry (including book burning in New Mexico)[3] came years before the final book, *Harry Potter and the Deathly Hallows*, was published and the dénouement known, whereas current Christians will have grown up with the *Narnia* books and so will 'know' that they are spiritually 'sound'!

Early on in the first book, *Harry Potter and the Philosopher's Stone*,[4] we are told that his mother Lily was prepared to and did in fact die, in order to protect her infant son. It was this act of self-sacrificial love which proved more powerful than the personification of evil in the person of Lord Voldemort, which caused his killing spell to rebound on him, almost destroying him, and depriving him of power and bodily form for a decade.

Harry is offered opportunities to use his magical powers for his own ends, but he remains pure of heart. What is reflected back at him in the mirror which shows the viewer's greatest desire is his dead family. This is in contrast to his friend Ron Weasley, who sees himself as school head boy and Quidditch sport captain holding competition cups. Harry could have entered Slytherin House, known for wizarding prowess and cunning, where he might have learned darker magic, but he recoiled from the idea in horror. He has involuntary insights into Voldemort's mind, a legacy of the attempt on his life. Harry is never tempted by the offer of power and influence for its own sake. When the replacement Minister for Magic, Rufus Scrimgeour, invites Harry to help with the Ministry's public relations and marketing, he declines, as what he is being asked to do isn't truthful. Like Jesus, Harry has his own temptations in an emotional desert and resists them.

Harry is stoic in the face of unjust treatment. This is especially demonstrated in his refusal to acknowledge the pain that Professor Umbridge inflicts on him when she is punishing him for declaring that Voldemort has returned and that he has seen and fought him. Umbridge is a colleague of Cornelius Fudge, Minister for Magic, and has been sent to spy for the Ministry within Hogwarts School. Harry also suffers repeatedly unfair treatment at the hands of Professor Severus Snape, who hated Harry's father and continually picks on Harry. Harry only retaliates occasionally, earning himself arduous detentions. Jesus had constant trouble with the Jewish authorities, the scribes and teachers of the Law. Harry's adoptive parents are spooked by the wizarding world and consider Harry if not mad then dangerously weird. Jesus' family went to collect him from his ministry as people thought he had gone mad.[5]

Another Christ-like characteristic of Harry Potter is his refusal to take revenge on his contemporary, Draco Malfoy. Malfoy perse-cuted Harry from his first day at school, seemingly jealous of his special status as 'the boy who lived'. He is a bully who is always accompanied by two thuggish, not too bright, schoolmates, acting as physical enforcers. Highly conscious of his own 'pure' wizarding blood line, Draco despises and insults those he deems to have been lesser born, particularly Harry's close friend Hermione. Draco's father Lucius is in league with Lord Voldemort and works to undermine the headmaster of Hogwarts, Professor Albus Dumbledore. In the final book, *Harry Potter and the Deadly Hallows,* Harry has opportunities to kill Draco but stays his hand, also forbidding others to kill him. He also does not allow friends of his parents to kill Peter Pettigrew, who betrayed them, when they have the chance, but wants him brought to trial. This is Jesus' command to 'Love your enemies, do good to those who hate you'[6] in action. Harry also manages ultimately to forgive Severus Snape, to the extent of naming his son Albus Severus, and describing Snape (on the last page in the last chapter of the last book) as 'probably the bravest man I ever knew'.

Harry is generous. He grew up with little, his adoptive parents keeping him short of food and material possessions while over-indulging their son Dudley. However, when he enters the wizarding world, Harry finds himself materially rich, his parents having left him a store of gold. He shares some of this good fortune with his friend Ron, who comes from an impoverished background, while taking care not to offend Ron's pride. Ron's twin elder brothers, Fred and George, long to set up a joke and magic shop, *Weasleys' Wizard Wheezes*, for which they are highly suited, but they have no financial capital. Harry unhesitatingly hands over his winnings from the Triwizard Tournament, to which he has never felt entitled, enabling them to go into business. Fred and George had been cheated earlier, when winning a bet on the Quidditch World Cup, by being paid in Leprechaun gold. This is indistinguishable from real gold, until it disappears after a couple of days. This idea is redolent of the devil's money in Michael Bulgakov's book, *The Master and Margarita*, which also vanishes.

Rowling has Harry subject to many of the negative as well as the positive life experiences encountered by Jesus. He suffers incomprehension and misunderstanding from his schoolmates, not to mention his human adoptive parents. He is accused of lying and attention seeking and gets a very bad press in the wizarding paper the *Daily Prophet*. He suffers nightmares, fears, feelings of inadequacy and yet has extraordinary powers which he uses for good. Within Harry Potter's world there is no person of God but the supernatural forces of magic can be used for both good and evil, in a similar way to Christians' experience of spiritual power. There is no one to whom Harry could pray, 'Abba, Father, for you all things are possible; remove this cup from me; yet, not what I want, but what you want.'[7] But his behaviour demonstrates that, however reluctantly, he accepts the role of saviour that is thrust upon him. He will have to suffer and be prepared to die. At the end of the sixth book, *Harry Potter and the Half-Blood Prince*, Harry stoically turns his face towards his task of finding and destroying the Horcruxes, objects which contain parts of Voldemort's soul, in order to defeat the power of evil. This is very much parallel to Jesus turning his face to Jerusalem for his final earthly journey, knowing that he will suffer and die in order to conquer the power of death.

Again, like Jesus, Harry experiences abandonment. Firstly he is orphaned, and so involuntarily abandoned, by the death of his parents when an infant. Shortly after he encounters his godfather Sirius Black,[8] who offers him a home away from the frightful Dursleys, Sirius is killed. Dumbledore, headmaster of Hogwarts School and his principal protector, dies, leaving him to continue his quest without that level of wizarding cover and support and, finally, his best friend Ron leaves him in limbo for a while, though Hermione sticks by him. Women stay at the Cross when the disciples abandon Jesus. When on the run from the Ministry of Magic and Voldemort's forces, with his wand broken and with no idea how to find the other Horcruxes, with Ron gone and just Hermione left,[9] Harry experiences what St John of the Cross describes as the *dark night of the soul*: complete spiritual abandonment with loss of purpose and meaning. For Jesus this occurred in Gethsemane, and he prayed, "'My Father, if it is possible, let this cup pass from me; yet not what I want but what you want." Then he came to the disciples and found them sleeping; and he said to Peter, "So, could you not stay awake with me one hour?"'[10] Psalm 22, part of which Jesus quotes while being crucified, also describes the sense of desolation, 'My God, my God, why have you forsaken me? Why are you so far from helping me, from the words of my groaning? O my God, I cry by day, but you do not answer; and by night, but find no rest.'

Eventually Harry returns to Hogwarts. He is hailed as a saviour and the expected leader in the imminent battle between forces loyal to (the now dead) Dumbledore and those in thrall to Voldemort. This is his triumphal entry, which he can't enjoy, as only he and his close friends know that he has a perilous quest searching for a shred of Voldemort's soul in a Horcrux which must be destroyed, without which no battle can be won.

When Harry learns from Snape's memories that Dumbledore viewed Harry and Voldemort as being so inextricably linked that the only way to defeat him would be for Harry to be prepared to die, he leaves the fighting at Hogwarts and walks with dread and longing for life, coupled with complete purposefulness, to what he believes will be his final destination. There, in the Forbidden Forest, he comes unarmed to Voldemort. This is his Gethsemane. In offering up his life as a ransom for many, Harry is not actually killed, though it was thought so by most of those present. His sparing of Draco Malfoy earlier ensures that the secret that he is still alive is kept by Draco's mother until he can finally defeat Voldemort.

When, in the last book, in a near-death experience Harry meets the dead Dumbledore, he says to Harry, 'You are the true master of death, because the true master does not seek to run away from death. He accepts that he must die, and understands that there are far, far worse things in the living world than dying.'[11] Harry offers his life up for the benefit of his world. You can't get a much more Christ-like attitude than that.

Hermione Granger

Hermione is in many ways an amalgam of the women who surrounded Jesus and those whom he encountered. She is a steadfast friend who never deserts Harry Potter. She is highly practical and always sets out to problem-solve, generally by looking things up in the library. This behaviour could be analogous to Martha's, who was the more practical if less spiritual of the two sisters. Martha's sister Mary sat at Christ's feet listening to his teaching, and Hermione is also prepared to learn from Harry. She suggests in *Harry Potter and the Order of the Phoenix* that he should teach 'Defence Against the Dark Arts' to selected students, as they are clearly getting nothing from the Ministry of Magic's stooge, Professor Dolores Umbridge. Hermione is also very bright, with a quick wit, like that of the Syro-Phoenician woman who asked Jesus to heal her daughter. This woman was not a Jew (Hermione is Muggle-born, a 'Mudblood'). When Jesus initially demurs, saying he has primarily come for the Jewish people, the children of Israel, and says to her, 'It is not fair to take the children's bread and throw it to the dogs,' she ripostes, 'Yet even the dogs eat the crumbs that fall from their master's table.'[12] (Possibly the wittiest comment in the Bible.) Hermione's natural instinct is to obey school rules but, as she perceives that breaking some of them would serve the greater good, she does so. Those women who followed Jesus, supporting and housing him, all risked scandal in their society, where women were primarily chattels, subject to the will of their fathers, husbands or brothers. They breached convention by behaving thus. These women were last at the Cross, first at the tomb and Mary Magdalene was the first to encounter the risen Christ and commanded to inform his disciples. Hermione demonstrates similar loyalty and risk-taking regarding Harry, whilst being brighter than most of her schoolmates, if at times a rather swotty know-all. Hermione also looks at the bigger picture, having the *Daily Prophet* wizarding newspaper delivered to school. Following the death of Lazarus, Martha accosts Jesus before he has reached their home claiming, 'Lord, if you had been here, my brother would not have died. But even now I know that God will give you whatever you ask of him.' Jesus said to her, 'Your brother will rise again.' Martha said to him, 'I know that he will rise again in the resurrection on the last day.'[13] Martha can see the bigger picture but has not yet fully understood that, as Jesus is the expected Messiah, he has power of life even after death.

Hermione demonstrates an admirable social conscience by striving to free the house-elves from what she deems to be slavery. They are totally subject to their wizard owners' wills, are not paid and can only be freed by being given proper clothes to wear. (There is the risk that were they to be free they then might have no access to employment or sustenance.) Hermione's school friends consider her to be wildly eccentric in this endeavour, although they partially come around to her way of thinking. She also displays compassion to the defenceless, for example by stopping the bullying by prefects of younger school children.

Finally, in an act of self-sacrifice, she has her parents transported to Australia and all memory of them having a daughter wiped from their minds. This was in order to protect them from Voldemort's Death Eaters, who would otherwise have kidnapped and tortured them in order to ascertain Hermione's whereabouts when she and Harry are on the run. The women who followed Jesus may well have found it hard to return home, having breached social convention by following and caring for him, rather than staying put and serving their closest male relatives. Jesus on the Cross hands over the responsibility of caring for his mother Mary to 'the disciple

Jesus loved' – probably John,[14] rather than to her immediate family. Tradition has it that Mary and John left Israel and spent time in Ephesus, in what is now Turkey.

Ron Weasley

Ron Weasley is somewhat analogous to 'the disciple that Jesus loved' in the Gospel according to John. He is loyal and brave, though lacking in self-confidence and feeling overshadowed by his five elder brothers. When he looks into the Mirror of Erised, which reflects back to you your heart's desire, he sees himself as a significant winner, head boy, Quidditch champion and in receipt of the symbols of status of which he so keenly feels the lack. Ron is occasionally reluctant to join in Harry's schemes; however, he was prepared to enter the Forbidden Forest with Harry following a trail of spiders despite being arachnophobic. He also is good at chess which comes in useful when having to play the wizards' version comprising life-size, animated and warlike pieces.[15] For a while, when Harry is dejected and depressed in his quest for the Horcruxes, Ron takes the lead, supporting him. His abandonment of Harry in *Harry Potter and the Deathly Hallows* is temporary and their friendship is restored.

Rubeus Hagrid

Hagrid is the huge Hogwarts gamekeeper, half giant, half human wizard. He displays many character traits of Jesus' disciple Simon Peter. Hagrid is honest, loyal, over-protective, and fearsomely strong. His heart is in the right place but he frequently puts his foot in his mouth. However, he is naïve, for example when buying a dragon's egg from a stranger in a pub. His behaviour is impulsive, occasionally over-emotional and prone to indiscretion, especially when in his cups. Peter gabbling away at the transfiguration, leaping overboard in the middle of a lake to greet Jesus, cutting off the High Priest's servant's ear and being filled with remorse at having denied Jesus, but becoming the rock on which the Church was built, are all types of behaviour one could associate with Hagrid.

Professor Albus Dumbledore

Dumbledore, the headmaster of Hogwarts, is in the tradition of mythical wizards. For example, Merlin in Sir Thomas Malory's *Le Morte d'Arthur* (the story of King Arthur and his Knights of the Round Table) and, more recently, Gandalf, in Tolkien's *The Hobbit* and *The Lord of the Rings*. Dumbledore is well aware of the tendency of power to corrupt, as was Gandalf, who never dared handle the ring, but had to give it to the Hobbits who were pure of heart. His counterpart, Sauron, goes the other way. The theme of corrupting power and its agent lodged in a golden ring goes back into legend beyond Richard Wagner's opera quartet, *Der Ring des Nibelungen*, known in English as the Ring cycle. In the Ring cycle, the gold forged into a ring will give you the power to rule the world, but to wield that power you must forever forego love, a theme which resonates within the Harry Potter universe.

In the final book Dumbledore reveals his early lust for power and the defeat of death which, in legend, would be achieved by combining the three Deathly Hallows, and how he realised how dangerous that would be. He paraphrases Plato[16] in saying to Harry, 'I had proven, as a very young man, that power was my weakness and my temptation. It is a curious thing, Harry, but perhaps those who are best suited to power are those who have never sought it. Those who, like you, have leadership thrust upon them, and take up the mantle because they must, and find to their own surprise that they wear it well.'[17] In Jungian terms, Dumbledore had come to terms with his *shadow side*, that part of our character, often hidden in our unconscious, which contains drives which we may find morally and socially unacceptable, but are still part of our make-up. By acknowledging his weakness for the abuse of power, he guards himself from acquiring too much of it.

Even so, Dumbledore tried on the Riddle family ring which contained one of the Deathly Hallows, the Resurrection Stone, which can bring back the semblance of a dead person. Perhaps he had hoped to see his mother and sister once again. This, even though he knew that Voldemort had turned the ring into a Horcrux by embedding a shred of his soul in it. Consequently, the ring contains such powerful curses that it withers Dumbledore's hand and he realises he is, from it, now under a slow sentence of death. He accelerates his demise by making himself available to Draco Malfoy to kill him but, knowing Draco would lose his nerve, instructs Snape to do the deed, thereby fulfilling Snape's 'unbreakable bond' which he swore to Draco's mother to support and protect the boy.

Apart from mythical wizards, Dumbledore shows some similarities to the character of the Christian 'God the Father'. Of course in Dumbledore's case he is neither the creator of the universe, nor is he omnipotent, omniscient, omnipresent nor immortal. Nevertheless he is a most powerful wizard who seems to know more of the wizarding universe than most, has wise insights, usually turns up when needed and is very old. His physical appearance is similar to Michelangelo's portrayals of God the Father on the ceiling of the Sistine Chapel, in Rome. Dumbledore acts as a spiritual father to Harry, periodically revealing the past and unfolding his situation to him. He allows Harry to engage with situations from which he would rather protect him, for example accompanying him to find the Horcrux lodged in the Slytherin locket.[18]

Dumbledore's magical powers exceed those of most other

wizards and he is the one wizard of whom Voldemort is afraid. He has an affinity with fire, setting a wardrobe alight to prove his wizarding credentials to the young Tom Riddle.[19] He also fights Voldemort with a fiery rope and uses fire as protection in the cave when securing the locket which they thought contained part of Voldemort's split soul. In the Old Testament, God appears to Moses as fire in the burning bush and as a pillar of fire leading the Israelites in the wilderness. He also sent down fire on Abraham's sacrifices and those of Elijah when he was contending with the priests of Baal.[20] Dumbledore's presence provides Harry and Hogwarts School with protection. He displays great wisdom and forbearance and unswervingly stands for what is right, true and good. He is unconcerned about purity of blood line but about what sort of character is developed by the choices a person makes. One can chose that which is right or be temped into choosing that which is easy. Jesus said, 'Enter through the narrow gate; for the gate is wide and the road is easy that leads to destruction, and there are many who take it. For the gate is narrow and the road is hard that leads to life, and there are few who find it.'[21] It is through the choices you make that your character is formed and your salvation may lie.

Professor Severus Snape

Snape is arguably the most complex and interesting character in the Harry Potter universe. His name contains echoes of his character, as do so many of Rowling's creations: Severus, redolent of 'severing', cutting, as his comments generally are, and 'severe', which his manner always is. Snape (a town in Suffolk) suggests 'snipe' which he does verbally all the time. He is introduced as a formidable teacher and Head of Slytherin house, whose pupils he shamelessly favours. He is thwarted through most of the saga in his desire to teach Defence Against the Dark Arts, which may be too close to home for Dumbledore's liking, having to settle for Potions Master, at which he also excels, having effectively rewritten the textbook, as emerges in *Harry Potter and the Half-Blood Prince*. He is an inventor/discoverer of spells such as *Sectumsempra* which, as its Latinate name suggests, means that the cut is for ever and cannot be healed. Poor George Weasley's ear succumbs to this curse.

I consider that there are parallels between Snape and St Paul. Paul (then known by his other name of Saul), initially persecuted Christians with great vigour. He was convinced he was doing what was right in God's eyes and zealously pursued his murderous regime. Snape followed Lord Voldemort in his initial rise to power (before Harry was born), becoming a Death Eater, having the Dark Mark etched on his forearm, and using his considerable wizarding talents and knowledge to that end. However, he seems to have had his own road to Damascus conversion and proceeded to change sides, working for the good even before Voldemort's initial downfall. Unfortunately, those unpleasant aspects of his conflicted personality remained fully exercised. What prompted his changing sides we only learn about in the last book but it involved Harry's mother Lily, the only person Snape ever loved. He had colluded with Voldemort to kill his rival in love, James Potter, but when Lilly is killed as well, Snape has an epiphany as to the reality and consequences of indulging Voldemort's type of evil. Love and grief cause his remorse, repentance and redemption.

Snape does not appear to have friends, doesn't wash his hair and keeps his study in a dungeon. He hates Harry which, given how Harry's father James bullied him at school, and the fact that he was in love with his mother Lily, is not surprising. (Harry looks like his father, but with his mother's eyes, which must have been a constant reminder to Snape of the humiliation he suffered and the loss he endured.) Snape had a deprived, neglected, even abused childhood. Alas, abused children often become abusive adults. His personality is very different from that of Harry, who also had a wretched upbringing, but developed into a well-balanced person. However, Snape does not become as depraved as Voldemort, who grew up unloved in an orphanage. St Paul's letters and various events in the Acts of the Apostles suggest that he, Paul, might have been rather hard to live with. Having travelled extensively, evangelising with Barnabas, Paul fell out with him over whether John Mark should accompany them. Rather than compromising, they split up.[22] Paul also had to relocate speedily after causing a riot. He could be manipulative, to the extent of exercising spiritual blackmail, as evidenced by his letter to Philemon.[23]

Once Voldemort returns, Snape acts as a double-agent, convincing Voldemort that he remains a loyal supporter and can be useful to him as a spy inside Hogwarts, whilst simultaneously assuring Dumbledore that he has reformed and can act as a source of information for him in order to undermine Voldemort's plans. Rowling keeps us in suspense as to which is Snape's true self until near the end of the last book. Initially this may not seem very Pauline but consider, 'I have become all things to all people, that I might by all means save some.'[24] Snape operates within the tension of deception which would put a strain on any person and Paul suppresses some of his beliefs so that he can reach others, whether in the Athens Areopagus or in the Jerusalem church. Snape is horrible to Harry throughout his schooldays. Harry always suspects the worst of him, seemingly justified when Snape appears to have murdered Dumbledore. However, secretly Snape repeatedly protects Harry. When Snape becomes headmaster in the final book, he also works to protect the students, while pretending to remain loyal to Voldemort, 'being all things to all men that some might be saved'. To the end Snape worked for the good and, as he lies dying, he offers Harry his memories which help him make sense of what has happened and which show Harry what he has to do to defeat Voldemort. Snape suffered, as Paul and Christ suffered, to promote the good in the teeth of opposition. As Snape died he gave Harry the means of gaining that victory. 'For to me, living is Christ and dying is gain.'[25]

Lucius Malfoy

Lucius Malfoy's names suggest aspects of his character. Malfoy derives from 'bad faith' in French, and indeed he acts in bad faith much of the time. Lucius, though different, suggests the name 'Lucifer'. Lucifer means 'light-bearer', described biblically as the 'morning star'. Lucifer is also one of the names for the Devil or Satan in the Bible. Although not all theologians agree that this passage refers to the Devil, the book of the prophet Isaiah states:

> How you are fallen from heaven, O Day Star, son of Dawn!
> How you are cut down to the ground, you who laid the nations low!
> You said in your heart, 'I will ascend to heaven; I will raise my throne
> above the stars of God; I will sit on the mount of assembly
> on the heights of Zaphon;
> I will ascend to the tops of the clouds,
> I will make myself like the Most High."
> But you are brought down to Sheol,
> to the depths of the Pit.'[26]

Lucifer's sin was to challenge the authority and supremacy of God. For this he was cast down, an event to which Jesus refers when addressing his disciples who had returned from healing the sick and casting out demons, 'I saw Satan fall like lightening from heaven. I have given you authority to trample on snakes and scorpions and to overcome all the powers of the enemy.'[27] Lucifer, aspiring to be like God, foreshadowed Adam and Eve doing the same when tempted by the serpent in the garden of Eden to eat fruit from the 'tree of the knowledge of good and evil' which God had forbidden them to touch. For this act of disobedience and on God's realisation that they would then be likely to eat the fruit of the 'tree of life', of immortality, enabling them to become like God, they were expelled from Paradise and had to work hard for a living.[28]

Lucius Malfoy is a class-conscious snob, contemptuous not only of half-bloods and Mudbloods, but also of the pure-blooded Weasley family who happen to be poor. Malfoy is redolent of old English families with French names who can trace their forebears back to the Norman conquest, feeling superior to the often red-headed and fecund Celtic fringe.

In Christian tradition, as exemplified by John Milton's *Paradise Lost*, Lucifer was the most beautiful of all the angels. 'But O how fall'n! how chang'd from him, who in the happy realms of light cloth'd with transcendent brightness didst out-shine myriads though bright.'[29] The fact that Lucius Malfoy is a pure-blood, handsome, blond, rich man ties in with this idea as well as with Jesus' description of Lucifer or Satan as being 'the prince of this world', a fallen star. However, it is Lord Voldemort who is the personification of evil in the Harry Potter universe.

As Voldemort's plans come to fruition, he moves into the Malfoy's manor house complete with albino peacocks, a symbol of pride in Christian iconography. Lucius and his wife Narcissa become more and more unhappy at this arrangement, as they see how sadistically Voldemort treats his enemies, feeding several of them to his pet snake Nagini.[30] One is reminded of the Duke of Buckingham in Shakespeare's play *Richard III*. Buckingham starts off as Richard's closest ally, helping him to become king, but baulks at cold-bloodedly murdering the young princes in the tower (one of whom had a better claim to the English throne than had Richard) and in the end Richard executes Buckingham.

Lord Voldemort

Formerly Tom Marvolo Riddle, also known as You-Know-Who, He Who Must Not Be Named, or the Dark Lord.

Tom Riddle did not have a good start in life. His witch mother from a pure-blood but perhaps somewhat inbred family was descended from one of the founders of Hogwarts School, Salazar Slytherin. By using magic she tricked a normal human/Muggle, Tom Riddle, into running off with her, but when she was pregnant she stopped supplying him with the magic potion, so he came to his senses and abandoned her. She gave birth to a boy, naming him Tom Riddle after his father and Marvolo after hers; shortly afterwards she died.[31] Tom grew up in a forbidding orphanage, despite the fact that he had a living father. A loveless start in life with little intimacy can damage a child's brain development, potentially leaving them unable to empathise with others. Rowling's description of Voldemort's character demonstrates the full spectrum of psychopathological traits. Robert D. Hare,[32] a researcher renowned in the field of criminal psychology, is Professor Emeritus of the University of British Columbia. He developed the Psychopathy Checklist (PCL) used to diagnose cases of psychopathy and it is also useful in predicting the likelihood of violent behaviour. Psychopaths may 'use charisma, manipulation, intimidation, sexual intercourse and violence' to control others and to satisfy their own needs. Hare states that, 'Lacking in conscience and empathy, they take what they want and do as they please, violating social norms and expectations without guilt or remorse.' He previously stated that, 'What is missing, in other words, are the very qualities that allow a human being to live in social harmony.'[33]

Voldemort, being a wizard possessed of exceptional magical powers, goes beyond human levels of psychopathology. He is set for world domination, encompassing the wizarding world, that of other magical creatures and also the world of Muggle humans. From early childhood he abused his powers, using them to bully his fellow orphans. The uncertainty over his origins and his loveless upbringing had left him with a sense of thwarted significance and social powerlessness, which he was determined to overcome. His greatest fear is that of death which he views as a failure. Tom Riddle, renaming himself Lord Voldemort, aspires to become immortal, as did Lucifer. In his first rise to power he set the primacy of pure-bloods over everything else, attracting support from many of the wizarding 'aristocracy'; ironic, given that he was a half-blood and illegitimate to boot. However, such behaviour is not unusual. People who are ashamed of or anxious about their past may project this antipathy onto others as a defence mechanism. They may also change their names to distance themselves from their origins or to promote a desired identity. Currently, the dictator of North Korea, Kim Jong-il, has himself referred to as the 'Dear Leader'. Also, there is some controversy about the legitimacy of Adolf Hitler's parents and his grandmother's name, Schicklgruber, could have been considered Jewish. However, going to school with the future philosopher Ludwig Wittgenstein may not have helped Hitler's self-esteem or fondness for Jews. His Nazi regime systematically murdered six million Jews and five million others, including gypsies, the mentally ill, the physically disabled, political opponents, Poles and homosexuals. Joseph Stalin's original name was Ioseb Besarionis dze Jughashvili. He adopted the name Stalin, which means 'man of steel'. He was Georgian and had a strong local accent, causing him to be viewed as a bit of a country bumpkin by his political opponents until it was too late. During his time in power as leader of the Soviet Union, from 1922 to 1953, he was responsible for the systematic death of some twenty million people. Being made to feel insignificant and powerless as a child can produce angry, bitter and vengeful adults, if compounding factors are present.

Apart from naming himself Lord Voldemort, which means 'flee

from death' (so striving for immortality), Riddle's name carried such power that he would be referred to by his enemies as 'He-Who-Must-Not-Be-Named'. Herodotus in 450 BC recorded that the Egyptian god of the dead, Osiris, was also referred to as 'He Who Must Not Be Named'. (Rowling may have known this or might have just tapped into an archetypal concept.) The idea of the power of a name goes back a long way. Biblically, knowing someone's name, calling them by name, is a powerful thing. At the burning bush when Moses asked God to tell him his name so he could demonstrate to the Israelites whose authority he had, God said to Moses, 'I AM WHO I AM', also translated as, 'I shall be whomever I shall choose to be'. He continued, 'Thus you shall say to the Israelites, 'I AM has sent me to you.'[34] In the prologue to John's Gospel he says of Jesus, 'But to all who received him, who believed in his name, [i.e. in him] he gave power to become children of God.[35] In Mark's Gospel it is primarily the demons which properly identify Jesus until the centurion at his crucifixion declares, 'Truly this man was God's Son!'[36] Some theologians believe that the demons were attempting to exert their influence over Jesus by naming him. There is power in a name.

Voldemort's striving for immortality caused him to attempt to split his soul into seven hidden parts by means of murder. In the Bible seven is a significant number signalling completion and so perfection. God created the universe in six days[37] and on the seventh day he rested.[38] It is symbolic that Voldemort tries to split his soul into seven parts.[39] (He unknowingly splits it into eight.)[40] He deconstructs his wholeness into the opposite of completeness. Atonement, 'at-one-ment', is what Jesus achieved for us on the Cross. We can become whole, deemed righteous by God, fully reconciled, our relationship restored with him as in the happiest of families: 'Ransomed, healed, restored, forgiven' in the words of the hymn.[41] Voldemort goes completely the other way in striving for immortality. As mentioned when describing Lucifer, he aims to become God's equal in power and instead becomes the person-ification of evil. In Harry he meets his match, as the power of love and self-sacrifice overcomes the power of evil. Dumbledore tells Harry, 'That which Voldemort does not value, he takes no trouble to comprehend. Of house-elves and children's tales, of love, loyalty and innocence, Voldemort knows and understands nothing. *Nothing.* That they all have a power beyond his own, a power beyond the reach of any magic, is a truth he has never grasped.'[42]

Voldemort murders Harry's parents in his attempt to assassinate him on 31 October, All Hallows Eve or 'Halloween', the night before the Church commemorates All Saints' Day. In Celtic tradi-tion it was considered a time when the boundary between the spiritual and material worlds is most porous, allowing both good and bad spirits to enter our world. Rowling won't have chosen this date by accident.

Voldemort's followers are called Death Eaters and have a Dark Mark burned onto their forearms showing to whom they belong. This is redolent of the followers of Satan, who are referred to as those who worship the beast, in the biblical book of Revelation:

> Those who worship the beast and its image, and receive a mark on their foreheads or on their hands, they will also drink the wine of God's wrath, poured unmixed into the cup of his anger, and they will be tormented with fire and sulphur in the presence of the holy angels and in the presence of the Lamb. And the smoke of their torment goes up forever and ever. There is no rest day or night for those who worship the beast and its image and for anyone who receives the mark of its name.[43]

The Dark Mark also has an unpleasant echo of Nazi concentration camp victims having identity numbers tattooed onto their forearms, as if they were pieces of property, which is how Voldemort treats his followers.

Cornelius Fudge

Fudge is the Minister for Magic. He is a classic caricature of the archetypal politician with a name to match, fudging every awkward issue. He unhesitatingly sacrifices truth on the altar of expediency. Conscious of his own shortcomings, he is envious of those with greater abilities and integrity, especially of Dumbledore. In the face of almost overwhelming evidence to the contrary, he strives to maintain the *status quo* by denying that Voldemort is back, that Harry fought him and that he has Voldemort's agents operating within the Ministry. He is in the pocket of Lucius Malfoy, a Death Eater, who can pay for Fudge's pet projects.[44] For Fudge, maintaining the apparent functioning of the Ministry of Magic and securing his place as its Minister trumps any evidence of a change in circumstances requiring a radical rethink of roles. Caiaphas, the High Priest in Jerusalem, operated in a similar way with Jesus. The idea that Jesus might be the long-expected Messiah was highly inconvenient to the smooth running of the Temple and to the position of the Jews as a subject nation under Roman rule. Caiaphas and his chief priests were blinded to all the signs Jesus gave that he was the Messiah, as he fulfilled prophecy after prophecy but didn't behave in the way they expected. They thought the Messiah would come with an earthly army to overthrow Roman rule. The fact that Caiaphas had completely missed the point of what he himself was there to do is paralleled by Fudge. Even when Fudge publicly admits Voldemort is back, he does too little too late.

Fudge is a snob, preferring pure-bloods to half-bloods or Muggles. Best of all are rich pure-bloods like the Malfoys. He continues to fawn on Lucius, long after he should have seen the danger signs. One of the difficulties that Caiaphas and the Temple elite had with Jesus was that he came not from a high-class family but was apparently the son of a provincial, small-town tradesman. Harry's announcement that Voldemort has returned is highly inconvenient to Fudge and to the smooth running of the Ministry of Magic. Consequently, Fudge tries to get Harry thrown out of Hogwarts and the wizarding world by accusing him of using magic inappropriately when fighting off attacking Dementors sent by his own organisation. (Dementors are creatures who suck all the joy out of people so they think they can never be happy again. At worst they can suck out your soul.) Harry is an embarrassment to Fudge, so he is prepared to act unjustly in order to get rid of him. One is reminded of Caiaphas' words regarding Jesus, 'It is better for you to have one man die for the people than to have the whole nation destroyed.'[45]

Peter Pettigrew ('Wormtail')

Peter Pettigrew was a friend, or more accurately a hanger-on, of Harry's father, James, and at school went around in a foursome with him, Sirius Black and Remus Lupin. When Harry's parents with the infant Harry went into hiding from Voldemort, Peter Pettigrew was made the 'Secret Keeper' of their protection spells. He held the key as to how to find them, although others thought it had been given to Sirius Black. Under pressure Pettigrew betrayed the Potters' location to Voldemort, who found them, killed Harry's parents but was unable to kill Harry as his mother Lily's loving self-sacrificial act caused the curse to rebound on Voldemort, almost destroying him. Harry was left with a lightening-shaped scar on his forehead and a sliver of Voldemort's soul within. So Harry and his parents were betrayed by a trusted friend, as good a parallel with Judas Iscariot as one might hope to find. Sirius Black was blamed for this deed which involved the death of several humans in the explosion and he was sent to the wizarding prison, Azkaban. When Harry is captured by Voldemort, Pettigrew is sent to kill him. Harry reminds him that he, Harry, had once saved his life and Pettigrew weakens in his resolve. At that moment his magical hand strangles him. Voldemort had fashioned it for him, following Pettigrew cutting off his own hand to add to the cauldron containing a human bone and Harry Potter's blood, so that Voldemort could gain a body.[46] Judas also repented and tried to give the Chief Priests back the money he had received for betraying Jesus. He then went out and hanged himself. [47]

The Dursleys

Harry's aunt, his mother's normal or 'Muggle' sister Petunia, and her irascible husband Vernon along with their spoilt and bullying son Dudley, are Harry's adoptive family. He was placed with them by Dumbledore when Harry's parents were killed. The Dursleys are an hysterically funny caricature of an appalling family, desperate to be considered 'normal'. Harry is a deep embarrassment to them, especially as his magical powers emerge. The Dursleys' desperation to maintain a genteel suburban respectability is thwarted by Harry's unconventionality. (Mind you, had their neighbours been aware that until he was eleven Harry was made to sleep in the under-stairs cupboard, rather than in one of the house's four bedrooms, as well as being underfed, their aura of respectability might have slipped.) Rowling has made this 'normal' family behave in exaggeratedly peculiar ways, whereas the wizarding fraternity are much more ordinary people, who can perform extraordinary acts. How Harry grows into the well balanced boy he becomes following this abusive upbringing is astonishing. He appears to have the ability to disengage and keep some semblance of sanity.

Draco Malfoy

The name Draco is the Latin *draco* meaning dragon or serpent. Draco is a thoroughly nasty piece of work, much like his father, Lucius. A natural bully, always accompanied by a couple of thuggish enforcers, he is particularly scathing of any Mudbloods and their friends, referred to as 'blood traitors'. Harry and Ron's friend Hermione, having non-wizarding parents, falls into this category. For protection Draco relies on his father's wealth, position as a Hogwarts School Governor and his influence with the Ministry of Magic. Draco is made a school prefect as the Ministry starts meddling with the running of the school and abuses his position by terrorising anyone within range. Eventually his arrogance is undermined as he sees his parents becoming pawns in Voldemort's power game, having offered their mansion as his headquarters. Draco can handle low-level bullying and violence but baulks at high-level torture and murder. Harry has several opportunities to kill him and stays his hand. At the end of the last book Draco seems to have mellowed. He is finally remorseful, taking a repentant route back to the world of goodness, a *prodigal son*.

Summary

Without being precisely a Christian allegory, Rowling's fictional characters display distinct parallels with biblical persons. They also find themselves in analogous situations. Harry himself is a Christ-like figure. He has a troubled infancy, surviving a murder attempt. He has unusual powers, is uncorrupted by temptations and witnesses to the truth. He is stoic in the face of unfair treatment, loyal to his friends and mentor and forgiving of his enemies. He has to cope with unlooked-for fame and notoriety, abandonment and imminent death. His destiny is to overcome evil by offering up his life as a ransom for many.

Hermione Granger is, in many ways, an amalgam of the women who surrounded Jesus and those whom he encountered, most notably the sisters, Martha and Mary, Mary Magdalene and the unnamed Syro-Phoenecian woman. She is a steadfast friend who never deserts Harry.

Rubeus Hagrid displays many character traits of Jesus' disciple Simon Peter. Hagrid is honest, loyal, impulsive, naïve, prone to indiscretion and fearsomely strong. His heart is in the right place but he frequently puts his foot in his mouth.

Professor Albus Dumbledore, Hogwarts' headmaster, is in the tradition of mythical wizards, and aware of power's tendency to corrupt. However, he is also analogous to the character of the Christian 'God the Father'. Of course he is neither the creator of the universe, nor is he omnipotent, omniscient, omnipresent nor immortal. Nevertheless, he is a most powerful, knowledgeable wizard, who has wise insights, usually turns up when needed and is very old.

Professor Severus Snape is, arguably, the most complex and conflicted character within the books. He has a Pauline–like conversion from serving evil to serving the cause of goodness. However, given his rough treatment of Harry, it is hard to see whose side he is on. Throughout the books he dissembles, 'being all things to all men that some might be saved'.

Evil is depicted in the character of Lord Voldemort, a once-powerful wizard who makes a renewed attempt to rule the world as the books proceed. He is aided by a 'prince' in this world, Lucius Malfoy. There are also characters reminiscent of Judas, Caiaphas, 'the disciple whom Jesus loved' and others.

2

World View

Harry Potter's world is radically different from ours in some important respects. Clearly our world does not have a group of people with the magical powers that the witches and wizards possess. I'm afraid we are all Muggles. Many of the magical creatures populating the books have come down to us through myth and folklore; centaurs who are half-man half-horse and mermaids arise in Classical Greece, leprechauns come from Ireland, goblins, trolls and elves from Germanic/Nordic legends and dragon stories stretch from Wales to China. All these and many others are magical archetypes which recur in tale-telling. There may be more things in heaven and earth than are dreamt of in our philosophy. The supernatural is an intrinsic part of Harry Potter's world. It is also intrinsic to the Christian viewpoint. God, the creator and sustainer of the universe is, among other things, a spiritual being. His Holy Spirit resides in Christians, and if they seek to be filled with his Spirit they may perform acts which, as yet, science is unable to explain.

There is another crucial difference between our world and that of Harry Potter. Any human being may become a Christian. It only requires a step of faith, a preparedness to engage with God through Jesus Christ and submit to his will. There is no barrier of birth, social class, intellect, race, colour or sex, 'There is no longer Jew or Greek, slave or free, there is no longer male and female for all of you are one in Christ Jesus.'[48] (Though not in the structures of much of his Church!) In the Harry Potter universe on the other hand, you either have magical powers or you do not; you cannot become a witch or wizard by trying. This is an important distinction when it comes to assessing whether the books would lead children into exploring the occult.

Authority

Rowling explores the concept of authority and its source. Is there an ultimate and overriding authority and, if so, from what does it derive? In Harry Potter's world, magic is a power which can be harnessed for good or ill. Of itself it is neutral and, like other human talents, some people are more gifted in one branch of magic or another, but all have to learn to develop and control their powers. The wizarding regulatory authority for the United Kingdom is the Ministry of Magic. It is a government seemingly of unelected members although there are mechanisms for removing the Minister. (S)he appears to have extensive executive powers. The Ministry includes: the Departments of Magical Law Enforcement, Transportation, International Magical Cooperation, Mysteries, Games and Sport and the Regulation and Control of Magical Creatures.

By the time Harry Potter is at school, the Ministry has forgotten that goodness, truth and justice should be the overriding principles of its operation and has been corrupted by individuals' lust for power and influence. This causes some Ministry officials to have a cavalier attitude to truth and justice, resulting in arbitrary court decisions and detentions without trial. The Minister, Cornelius Fudge, is vain and insecure and ignores evidence that Voldemort has returned and that his Ministry has been infiltrated by Death Eaters. Some Ministry officials are even nastier, with Dolores Umbridge being thoroughly sadistic.[49] There are others working in the Ministry who continue to operate in an honest and fair manner, for example, Ron's father, Arthur Weasley. Rowling demonstrates that even if institutions start off with the best of intentions, they tend to get bogged down in bureaucracy, inefficiency and infighting, distorting their aims and output. A useful lesson to learn early.

Dumbledore and Harry fall foul of the Ministry as their insistence that Voldemort has returned challenges the *status quo* and is potentially disruptive to the smooth but complacent running of the Ministry. Harry has Dementors[50] set on him by Umbridge and is then summoned to a rigged trial, as he has used magic illegally out of school to defend himself and his cousin Dudley Dursley from them. Only Dumbledore, by finding a witch witness and defending him himself, saves Harry from being expelled from Hogwarts and the wizarding world.[51]

Jesus had much the same effect on the Jerusalem Temple authorities. As a whole, the formal religious hierarchy of the Temple didn't recognise Jesus' direct line to the higher authority of God, as demonstrated in the scriptures, because they had distorted and obscured the sentiments of justice, truth and mercy with a tangle of legalisms.

When Jesus was teaching and a paralysed man was lowered through the roof, Jesus told him his sins were forgiven. The scribes thought he was blaspheming so Jesus, realising this, said, 'Which is easier, to say, "Your sins are forgiven, or to say, Stand up and walk? But so that you may know that the Son of Man has authority on earth to forgive sins" – he then said to the paralytic – "Stand up, take your bed and go to your home." And he stood up and went to his home.'[52] Jesus was also accused of using spiritual power supplied by the devil, Beelzebul. His response was: 'If I cast out demons by Beelzebul, by whom do your own exorcists cast them out? Therefore they will be your judges. But if it is by the Spirit of God that I cast out demons, then the kingdom of God has come to you.'[53] There were many occasions where Jesus' authority was challenged and he repeatedly pointed towards the *spirit* of the Law rather than the legalistic rules.

Once, when Jesus entered the Temple, the chief priests and the elders of the people came to him as he was teaching, and said:

> By what authority are you doing these things, and who gave you this authority?' Jesus said to them, 'I will also ask you one question; if you tell me the answer, then I will also tell you by what authority I do these things. Did the baptism of John come from heaven, or was it of human origin?' And they argued with one another, 'If we say, "From heaven," he will say to us, "Why then did you not believe him?" But if we say, "Of human origin," we are afraid of the crowd; for all regard John as a prophet.' So they answered Jesus, 'We do not know.' And he said to them, 'Neither will I tell you by what authority I am doing these things.'[54]

The Temple authorities didn't want to recognise who Jesus was, as the return of the Messiah in such an unlikely form would severely disrupt their power in the operation of the Temple and of the Jewish state under Roman rule. However, some senior members of the Council and Pharisees believed in Jesus, for example Joseph of Arimathea and Nicodemus.

Both Harry and Jesus are punished for pointing to the truth. In Harry's case it is that evil has re-entered the world, whereas in Jesus' case it is that he, 'the way, the truth and the life' has arrived!

Death, bereavement and the afterlife

The theme of death, how it affects those left behind, how they deal with their grief and what there might be beyond death run through all the Harry Potter books. Some critics have thought that these are unsuitable subjects for children's literature, but how else are they to begin to think about and process our ultimate end, if it is sanitised out of their experience? Children are exposed in the visual media to much violence, whether on TV, in the cinema or in video-games. Whereas, in reading about these subjects, they can set their own pace, put the book down and even consult an adult, in order to manage their exposure and to place it into context. Many people in our society have little experience of death, as our elderly and seriously sick tend to be tidied away in hospitals and hospices. The shock of a young death we view as an affront to the natural order of things. The developing world, alas, has more experience of the latter and tends to care for its dying elderly in their communities, so death is less of a taboo subject.

Death

Harry Potter experienced death in his infancy, his parents having been wiped out by Lord Voldemort. When Harry is faced with a Dementor, which evokes his worst memory, he hears a woman screaming, which he recognises as his mother's last sound. He grows up to the age of eleven believing that his parents died in a car crash until Hagrid turns up and informs him of his wizarding identity and heritage. Harry's grief for the absence of his parents is that the opportunity to know them has been forever lost. He becomes aware that in the wizarding world he is a celebrity, known as 'the boy who lived', which he finds hard to handle. Harry then experiences Cedric Diggory being murdered next to him, while he only just escapes. Following this, having encountered his godfather, Sirius Black, whom he is only just getting to know and who has offered him a home away from the frightful Dursleys, he experiences the devastating shock of seeing Sirius killed by Bellatrix Lestrange. Subsequently Dumbledore is seemingly murdered, dying near the end of the sixth book, *Harry Potter and the Half-blood Prince*. Finally, the house-elf Dobby, whom Harry freed from servitude in the Malfoy household, is killed trying to save him. (All this before the Battle of Hogwarts.)

Bereavement and ways of grieving

Rowling, through Harry and Cedric's girlfriend Cho Chang, accurately describes the way teenagers in particular deal with bereavement. To quote the article, 'Controversial Content – Is Harry Potter harmful to Children?' By Deborah J. Taub and Heather L. Servaty-Seib:

> 'Harry expresses and exhibits symptoms and behaviour common for bereaved teenagers. His responses are often multifaceted and include shock, numbness, blame and guilt, sadness, and rage. More specific to being a teenager, Harry is actively reluctant to discuss his grief, particularly following the deaths of Cedric and Sirius. He appears to camouflage his grief, which is common for bereaved teenagers who are working to fit in and minimize any differences that may exist between them and their peers ... Although this behaviour is motivated by a desire to belong, it often results in young people not having opportunities to process their experiences with others ... Harry also seems to struggle with the idea that anyone can understand his feelings – another common experience for teenagers in general ... In particular, when Dumbledore attempts to normalize Harry's pain following Sirius' death by indicating that he knows how Harry feels', Harry explodes in rage. (*Harry Potter and the Order of the Phoenix*, Chapter 37.)[55]

Cho Chang deals with her grief over Cedric's death quite differently from Harry. She is inconsolably weepy and wants to talk about Cedric repeatedly. She latches on to Harry but it is not so much that she is attracted to him, but that she wants to re-live Cedric's last moments which only Harry witnessed. Harry finds this oppressive and hard to understand, as he grieves quite differently.

Neville Longbottom's parents are alive, but were tortured into madness by the Cruciatus curse being repeatedly used on them and are incarcerated in St Mungo's hospital. Neville never speaks about his parents and offers no explanation as to why he is being brought up by his grandmother, but then no one has ever thought to ask him. However, he becomes violent towards Draco Malfoy when he is teased about the Cruciatus curse.

I believe it will be helpful for readers of the books to be exposed to all these bereavement styles so that, were they then to suffer their own bereavement, they would know that it is OK to feel this way and might be able to gain appropriate support. They would also be better prepared to support others who are grieving.

Importance of ritual

Various post-death rituals are performed in the books. Harry finds that physically digging the house-elf Dobby's grave with a spade, rather than by magic, is cathartic. Luna then says some words over it and Harry carves a gravestone with the epitaph '*Here lies Dobby – a Free Elf*'. Physical actions, a eulogy and epitaphs all play a part in making concrete the reality of death, helping people come to terms with it. Harry himself did not emotionally engage with Dumbledore's funeral, which seemed to have little bearing on the man he knew. There might have been others at that more formal occasion who did relate to it. The awfulness of not having a body to bury comes across with the deaths of Sirius and Mad-Eye Moody. For some it can be harder to obtain closure in such circumstances. Rowling covers this whole range of experiences, demystifying our society's death taboo in what I consider to be a helpful manner.

The afterlife

Within the Potter universe there are several aspects to the idea of

35

an afterlife. Firstly we encounter assorted ghosts in Hogwarts. Each house seems to have a pet one, Gryffindor's being Nearly Headless Nick. (When Hermione, ever the logical one, asks him how he can be nearly-headless, he tips his head almost off. She then rather wishes she hadn't.) Nick's great regret is that his barely attached head means he can't join the 'Headless Hunt', which gallops on horseback through the school at intervals. These ghosts seem to be dead people who are afraid to go on to a full afterlife, but just hang around in limbo with the living. When Sirius is killed, Harry is told that he will not come back as a ghost, but has gone on. There are also what are referred to as Inferi. These are dead people whose bodies can be taken over and controlled by dark magic. In the lake separating the island where Voldemort hid a Horcrux and the land, the water is filled with Inferi who pull to their death by drowning anyone who touches the water. They are similar to the idea of zombies.[56]

In *Harry Potter and the Goblet of Fire*, when Harry is in the grave-yard, being challenged to a duel to the death by Voldemort, their spells collide and their wands connect with a beam of golden light which forms a lattice-like cage around the two of them. Then, apparitions of those Voldemort has killed, including Harry's parents, come out of his wand. They can speak to Harry, telling him what to do and Cedric's asks Harry to take back his body to his parents. They hold off the forces of evil for the few seconds it is necessary for Harry to reach the Portkey and return to Hogwarts. Harry also conjures up shades of his parents, Sirius and Lupin, by using the Resurrection Stone for the first and last time, so they can accompany him on his walk into the Forbidden Forest, to what he believes will be his willing death in order to defeat Voldemort.

Deep in the Ministry of Magic, on the level of the Department of Mysteries, there is a cavern with a stone arch which has a tattered curtain or veil hanging from it.[57] Harry and his companions can hear voices seemingly coming from the other side but can walk around the arch and still only see the veil. They are then attacked by Death Eaters. Sirius and others come to the rescue and when Bellatrix Lestrange kills Sirius with the curse of *Avada Kedavra*, he falls though the arch, past the veil and vanishes from sight. He is truly dead, but the presence of the voices indicates that there is a life beyond physical death.

At the moment when Jesus died on the Cross, defeating death and asking forgiveness for his killers and tormentors, the curtain in the Temple was torn in two.[58] Christians have a sure and certain hope of the afterlife. As St Paul said, 'If you declare with your lips that Jesus is Lord and believe in your heart that God raised him from the dead, you will be saved.'[59] 'No eye has seen, nor ear heard, nor the human heart conceived, what God has prepared for those who love him.'[60] 'No, in all these things we are more than conquerors through him who loved us. For I am convinced that neither death, nor life, nor angels, nor rulers, nor things present, nor things to come, nor powers, nor height, nor depth, nor anything else in all creation, will be able to separate us from the love of God in Christ Jesus our Lord.'[61]

There is one more puzzling encounter with death when Harry, who has been struck by a supposed killing spell from Voldemort, has a near-death experience, meeting the dead Dumbledore. In it Dumbledore is able to explain various events to Harry, clarifying to him that, having been prepared to die, he hasn't actually done so, though he now has the choice to move on to death or return to life. Harry chooses to go back, on order to finish his task of defeating Voldemort. Harry asks Dumbledore, 'Is this real or has this been happening inside my head?' Dumbledore replies, 'Of course it is happening inside your head, Harry, but why on earth should that mean it is not real?'[62]

The nearest Christian equivalent to Harry's experience is recorded by St Paul in his second letter to the Corinthians. Referring to himself in the third person he writes, 'I will go on to visions and revelations of the Lord. I know a person in Christ who fourteen years ago was caught up to the third heaven, whether in the body or out of the body I do not know; God knows. And I know that such a person . . . was caught up into Paradise and heard things that are not to be told, that no mortal is permitted to repeat.'[63]

Life worse than death

Voldemort is striving for immortality as he perceives death to be a failure. He can conceive of nothing worse than death, but, alas, he lacks those attributes of humanity which make life worth living, such as love and relationships. He fractures his soul, attempting to gain everlasting life, but just achieves long-term existence until all the portions of his soul contained in him and the Horcruxes are destroyed. The Philosopher's Stone in the first book will enable the holder to create the elixir of life, protecting them from death (but not necessarily old age). When Nicholas Flamel and his wife agree to give it up to destroy the stone's potency they are already over 650 years old. Rowling's Dementors epitomise what may make life bearable or not worth living. In their presence a person's worst memories are recalled and they feel despair, desolation and that they will never be happy again. This is the most succinct description of clinical depression I have encountered. If Dementors are allowed to, they will 'kiss' an individual whose soul is then sucked out of them forever, leaving an animate husk with all that makes life worth living removed. There are greater things to fear than death.

Jesus said, 'For those who want to save their life will lose it, and those who lose their life for my sake will find it. For what will it profit them if they gain the whole world but forfeit their life? Or what will they give in return for their life?'[64]

For the greater good

Rowling engages with the value system of Utilitarianism, associated with the philosophy of John Stewart Mill.[65] As its name suggests, it values people and social structures primarily on the basis of their utility, their usefulness. Ideally, actions should bring the greatest amount of benefit or pleasure to the greatest number of people. Unfortunately, human nature being what it is, those governing using this principle seem to reap the benefits at the expense of the governed. When as young men Dumbledore and his friend Gellert Grindelwald look to their futures, Grindelwald wants to have wizards rule the world not just of witches and wizards but of Muggles and all sentient creatures, as they are obviously so much better suited to doing so than anyone else. There is a seductive logic in this which at first attracts Dumbledore, especially as the two of them are clearly the most gifted wizards of their generation. The letter the seventeen-year-old Dumbledore wrote to Grindelwald attempting to set limits on the means to reach the justified ends of the *Greater Good* reads as follows:

> *Gellert –*
>
> *Your point about wizard dominance being FOR THE MUGGLES' OWN GOOD – this, I think, is the crucial point. Yes, we have been given power and, yes, that power gives us the right to rule, but it also gives us responsibilities over the ruled. We must stress this point, it will be the foundation stone upon which we build. Where we are opposed, as we surely will be, this must be the basis of all our counter-arguments. We seize control FOR THE GREATER GOOD. And from this it follows that where we meet resistance, we must use only the force that is necessary and no more. (This was your mistake at Durmstrang! But I do not complain, because if you had not been expelled, we would never have met.)* Albus[66]

However, Dumbledore gradually disagrees with Grindelwald and things become very nasty. Dumbledore's young sister gets caught up in this row. She had been permanently damaged by having been assaulted by some boys when seven years old and cannot control her magic. The ensuing fight between the boys leaves her dead, neither boy knowing whose spell had inadvertently killed her. Dumbledore realises the dangers of reaching for absolute power, even if you think you are the best person to wield it (perhaps especially if you think that), as he recognises how, in the words attributed to Lord Acton, 'power tends to corrupt and absolute power corrupts absolutely'.

Hermione and Harry also use the phrase 'for the greater good' when contemplating breaking school roles in order to fight Voldemort. However, they are not set on world domination.

Various colonial and political regimes have justified the dominance of one group of people over another, often a minority over a majority, on the basis that they know best and can run a regime of economic and political competence, imposing the rule of law. When one views how countries have been managed once their colonial masters have been overthrown, one can see that the former rulers had a point, as often the new regime supports cronyism, (where you give the top jobs and contracts to your family, friends, clan and tribe rather than to more able and qualified people). Often corruption, including bribery, also flourishes in these regimes. However, just because indigenous people will need perhaps several centuries to achieve what the developed world thinks of as an appropriate political system (as the developed world did in the past), it is not a sufficiently valid reason for denying national autonomy. Instead, the developed world should help by education and example, rather than by exploitation.

Anti-racism

Rowling provides a devastating critique of racism in her treatment of wizarding blood lines and people's attitudes to them. There are the pure-bloods, whose ancestors were all witches and wizards; half-bloods, where one parent had magical powers; and Mudbloods, a witch or wizard offspring of normal, human, 'Muggle' parents. The most humiliating thing to be born as is a 'Squib', a non-magical person born of wizarding parents. (Non-academic children of intellectuals can have similar problems in our society.) 'Blood traitors' are pure or half-bloods who consort with Muggles. One aspect of Voldemort's original rise to power was his attempt to assert the superiority of pure-bloods to the detriment of all other wizards, witches, magical creatures and ordinary human beings. This apartheid was initially attractive to many, who were later horrified by how it developed into persecutions and massacres. Others stuck with their notion of their blood line superiority and remained Voldemort's supporters, called 'Death Eaters', until they were overthrown and jailed or recanted after Voldemort was almost destroyed when his killing spell aimed at Harry rebounded on him. The Malfoys physically resemble the aristocratic Aryan ideal and they despise the Weasleys, ostensibly for liking Muggles, thereby being blood traitors, as well as for being poor. The fact that the Weasleys all have red hair and have produced lots of children is redolent of the Roman Catholic Irish, who have also been looked down on over the years as feckless by the high-class protestant English. Thus Rowling exposes social class prejudice.

In the Muggle world, Vernon Dursley's sister, Marjorie, insults Harry by comparing his mother with a rogue bitch who will produce renegade puppies. This so incenses Harry that he inadvertently causes her to blow up like a balloon and float away!

The world has seen many variants on this theme of belief in racial or ethnic superiority, all of them evil. In Nazi Germany, the cult of the supposed superiority of a pure-blood Aryan race led to the genocide in concentration camps – not merely of six million Jews, but also of five million gypsies, homosexuals, the mentally ill, political opponents, Poles and other 'undesirables'. In apartheid South Africa, it was illegal for black and white people to intermarry. They lived in separate locations, attended separate schools and a white minority held all the wealth, political and judicial power until that system was dismantled, and free multiracial elections were held in 1994.

There were of course racial and political divisions in Jesus' day. Politically, being a Roman citizen came with privileges and access to power. Religiously, ethnically, you were either a Jew or you weren't; though conversion was possible. However, the tracing of your ancestors back to the sons of Jacob awarded status. Hence Paul declaring, 'If anyone else has reason to be confident in the flesh, [i.e. in my Jewish pedigree] I have more: circumcised on the eighth day, a member of the people of Israel, of the tribe of Benjamin, a Hebrew born of Hebrews; as to the law, a Pharisee; as to zeal, a persecutor of the church; as to righteousness under the law, blameless.'[67] Paul goes on to say that he considers these qualifications worthless because of the surpassing value of know-ing Jesus Christ. Jews often despised Gentiles and many Gentiles were baffled and exasperated by the attitude of Jews. Jesus' minis-try, although primarily to the children of Israel, was extended to Samaritans, Greeks of the Decapolis and even to the slave of a Roman centurion.

Rowling has offered a strong strand of combating racism in the Harry Potter novels. The names of various Hogwarts pupils indicate ethnic diversity, for example, Lee Jordan (who wears his hair in dreadlocks), Cho Chang and the twin sisters Pavati and Padma Patil. Kingsley Shacklebolt, who is in the Order of the Phoenix, is black.

Hermione is the real consciousness raiser, aiming to free the house-elves from effective slavery. However, Harry also treats elves, goblins, centaurs and hippogriffs with a respect they were unused to from wizards. We are asked to consider how we treat sentient creatures whom we assume are here for our benefit, whether pets, farmed or wild animals, in or out of zoos.

Gender equality

Although most of the leading characters are male, women and girls play a full part in every aspect of life in the wizarding world. Two of Hogwarts' four founders were women and it has had headmistresses. At the school the sexes have equal status. The key sport is Quidditch, a rumbustious and complex bat and ball game played on flying broomsticks by mixed-sex teams. This is similar in our world to the equestrian sports of show-jumping, three-day eventing and, to a lesser extent, horse racing, where horse-riding women compete on equal terms with men. (Clearly it helps to have a mount!) Hermione, Harry and Ron's close friend, is the most accomplished wizarding pupil in the school and has a forensic brain as well as being emotionally sensitive and mature. Professor Minerva McGonagall is Deputy Headmistress and the Ministry of Magic contains senior witches. Our world, not to mention the Church, is less egalitarian.

No underage sex, drink or drugs

The Harry Potter books contain no underage sexual activity, drinking of alcohol, smoking or illegal drug taking. Mind you, given the nature of the potions they can concoct, our drugs of choice seem rather tame! While school age, the children never get beyond kissing or 'snogging', as it is referred to, butterbeer seems no more potent than Coca-Cola, recreational drugs and smoking are never mentioned.

Professor Trelawney, the dippy Divinations teacher, has a sherry habit, but that is portrayed as part of her inability to cope.

In terms of sexual morality, Tom Riddle, who renames himself Lord Voldemort, was born out of wedlock through deception and ended up in an orphanage, even though he was not an orphan but had a living father. None of this is put forward as a good start in life.

Family values

The Dursleys, Harry's aunt and uncle, his adoptive parents, live at 4 Privet Drive, Little Whinging, Surrey; the ultimate parody suburban address. They have a detached house in a nice street, with a smart car and a tidy garden. They cultivate an aura of conventional respectability, while being terrified that Harry will blow it by being weird. The Dursleys seem to have plenty of money and spoil their son Dudley with mountains of presents and treats (while treating Harry abominably). However, Dudley isn't happy, eats too much and runs a gang at school terrorising anyone within range.

The wealthy and pure-blood wizards, the Malfoys, have only one son, Draco. Despite his advantages he is not comfortable in his own skin and runs a bullying gang at Hogwarts, while not seeming to have any real friends. He appears lonely and is derogatory about anyone not as 'aristocratic' i.e. as pure-blood as himself, seemingly as a defence mechanism.

The Weasley wizarding family, on the other hand, are always short of funds. Mr Weasley has a presumably not very well paid job in the Ministry of Magic and they have produced a large brood of six sons and, finally, one daughter. Although they experience the usual strains and tensions of a large family containing strong characters, it is essentially a happy and supportive home in which all the children have been in receipt of much love from their parents, Arthur and Molly. It is Harry's first taste of what it is like to live in a healthy family. Despite having to contend with second-hand and cast-off clothes, pets and books, the children all turn out to be reasonably well balanced and decent individuals. An indication of their real concerns is Molly's clock which, rather than telling the time, contains hands representing each member of her family, pointing to their whereabouts and even indicating if they are in mortal danger.

The first place that Harry ever felt was home was Hogwarts School. Here he finds companionship, support and nurturing for the first time in his life. He gains a father figure in Dumbledore and sibling equivalents in Hermione and Ron. The best sort of colleges and institutions can do this, to the benefit of all concerned.

Rowling clearly emphasises that it is in the qualities of parenting and unconditional love, not in material possessions, that happy families are made. Molly's worst fear, as demonstrated by her Boggart's manifestation, is of her family being injured or killed. Protective and loving friendships and relationships abound in Rowling's books.

The Bible is remarkably short on detail of what we would now consider to be well balanced families offering a supportive upbringing. When Cain killed Abel, Adam and Eve must have wondered where they went wrong. The favouritism shown to Joseph by his father Jacob generated jealousy in his brothers. That, and his tactless recounting of prophetic dreams, almost cost him his life at their hands. The Patriarchs tended to be polygamous and the Kings had many wives and concubines. Rebellious children could be stoned to death![68]

We know little of Jesus' family life apart from references to the existence of brothers and sisters. The only incident recorded, once he was beyond infancy, was his staying behind in Jerusalem after the Passover and his parents returning there to search for him, finding him only after three days. They were worried sick and were understandably furious when they caught up with him debating in the Temple. His insouciance must have been maddening:

> When his parents saw him they were astonished; and his mother said to him, "Child, why have you treated us like this? Look, your father and I have been searching for you in great anxiety." He said to them, "Why were you searching for me? Did you not know that I must be in my Father's house?" But they didn't understand what he said to them.[69]

The household of Martha, Mary and Lazarus seems to be mutually supportive but even there, jealousies and tensions emerge, for example when Mary is sitting listening to Jesus, leaving Martha to do all the work. Presumably their parents are dead and Lazarus is under-age, or the Bible would have told us that Jesus went to his house, rather than to Martha's.[70]

Ideally the Church family should provide those protective, supportive and loving friendships and relationships for all, especially where people have been less than lucky with their own families.

Celibate school staff

All the Hogwarts School staff are unmarried. We get some hints of love interests; for example Snape was in love with Harry's mother Lily, but she fell for James. Remus Lupin marries Tonks only after he has left Hogwarts and Hagrid's dalliance with Madam Maxine, the giant Headmistress from the French school, comes to little. There are no intimations in the books concerning Dumbledore's sexuality apart, perhaps, from his flamboyant choice of robes; however, according to the BBC online news channel:[71]

Harry Potter author J.K. Rowling has revealed that one of her characters, Hogwarts school headmaster Albus Dumbledore, is gay. She made her revelation to a packed house in New York's Carnegie Hall on Friday, as part of her US book tour. She took audience questions and was asked if Dumbledore found 'true love'. 'Dumbledore is gay,' she said, adding he was smitten with rival Gellert Grindelwald, whom he beat in a battle between good and bad wizards long ago. The audience gasped, then applauded. 'I would have told you earlier if I knew it would make you so happy', she said. 'Falling in love can blind us to an extent,' she added, saying Dumbledore was 'horribly, terribly let down' and his love for Grindelwald was his 'great tragedy'.

This revelation was greeted in predictable fashion by those on both sides of the homosexuality debate. Gay rights activists were sorry that Rowling hadn't made Dumbledore's sexuality explicit in the books and some of the conservative Christian Right denounced the Harry Potter series all over again, having previously just got worked up regarding witchcraft. For the latter, the fact that Dumbledore is celibate is neither here nor there. Holiness of life seems to pass them by. Perhaps they should re-read the Gospels as Jesus said it is by the fruit of our lives, the outcome of our words and actions, that we will be judged, not our innate tendencies.[72]

School discipline

These days, the behaviour expected of the pupils at Hogwarts, and the discipline exerted to ensure it, would be every schoolteacher's dream. Rudeness and insolence are not tolerated. Pupils are expected to be prompt for lessons, with their books, and to pay attention. Homework must be handed in on time. Sanctions are sufficient to maintain an orderly environment. Prefects also have organisational and disciplinary roles. Of course these powers are abused occasionally but the behavioural ideal is made very clear.

Study and homework

Although the wizarding community has special powers, these have to be honed and trained in order to develop and control them, much as we have to in order to develop our potential. Hogwarts imposes a heavy academic load and the pupils don't have the world-wide web from which to crib answers (as if!). Exams, and the terror they induce, turn up every year. (In terms of terror, Hermione is the exception. She loves exams and is mortified when some are cancelled.)

Healthy competition

The four school houses are proud of their respective heritage and keen to win the House Cup by gaining the maximum number of House Points over the term. Winning the Quidditch competition for the House brings much glory and jubilation. The houses attract pupils with different characteristics as enumerated by the Sorting Hat which allocates first-years to the houses. Part of its song goes:

> You might belong in Gryffindor,
> Where dwell the brave at heart,
> Their daring, nerve and chivalry
> Set Gryffindors apart;
> You might belong in Hufflepuff,
> where they are just and loyal,
> Those patient Hufflepuffs are true
> And unafraid of toil;
> Or yet in wise old Ravenclaw,
> If you've a ready mind,
> Where those of wit and learning
> Will always find their kind;
> Or perhaps in Slytherin

You'll make your real friends,
Those cunning folk use any means
To achieve their ends.[73]

Rowling makes clear that she values all these virtues except for Slytherin's Machiavellian streak. The risk of sorting such like-minded/talented children into separate houses is that healthy competition can spill over into unhealthy rivalry. Eventually the Slytherins have to decide just who's side they are on.

Obeying and disobeying rules

One criticism of Harry Potter is that he has a cavalier attitude to school rules, just like his father. Generally this is only when Harry is striving for the greater good and engaging with events which the rule-book doesn't cover. His breaches for his own advantage seem only to occur when he considers he has been unjustly treated, for example when his uncle failed to sign a form allowing him to visit the wizarding village of Hogsmead. Jesus had similar run-ins with the religious authorities of his day. His healing on the Sabbath got up the nose of the priests and scribes every time.

Dumbledore offers Harry the choice of doing that which is right or that which is easy. Jesus said, 'Enter through the narrow gate; for the gate is wide and the road is easy that leads to destruction, and there are many who take it. For the gate is narrow and the road is hard that leads to life, and there are few who find it.'[74]

Complexity and contrariness of human nature

Rowling creates three-dimensional, believable characters containing contradictions. Good-looking people aren't necessarily good, ugly people aren't automatically bad, though both can be. In fact the black and white dualism which many fairy stories employ is shown in Harry Potter to be an over simplistic view of human nature. We all contain light and darkness and which choices we make, how we behave, is more important than our starting position. Sirius Black, Harry's father's great friend and Harry's godfather, is essentially a decent man, but treats his house-elf abominably, as if the creature (insultingly named Kreature) has no feelings, which he clearly has. Dolores Umbridge, the Ministry stooge sent to Hogwarts, has a saccharine-sweet demeanour, but is a vicious sadist.[75] James, Harry's father, was an arrogant show-off and a bully, which is partly why Snape shows such antipathy towards Harry. Snape doesn't wash his hair, picks on Harry in class and favours his House, Slytherin, with House Points. However he secretly protects Harry from harm. Mundungus Fletcher is a good-hearted wizard but also a coward and a petty criminal. Hermione's swottiness is both a help and a hindrance to her social relationships. Gilderoy Lockhart, the impossibly handsome, conceited and boastful Professor of Defence Against the Dark Arts, whose apparent magical achievements, as recorded by him, are built on a sham, is the one character that in an interview Rowling said was based on a real person (whom she refused to name). One is reminded of the song, 'You're so vain, you probably think this song is about you. You're so vain'.[76] I certainly have met some like him. These character sketches are all useful lessons for life.

Facing and overcoming fear

Rowling describes a shape-shifting creature she calls a Boggart, which hides in enclosed spaces and manifests itself as one's worst fear. A Boggart (also Bogart), according to the *Shorter Oxford English Dictionary*, is something which frightens the horses. Rowling's version is similar to Room 101 in George Orwell's book, *Nineteen Eighty-Four*, where you are faced with your greatest terror. This was used to interrogate and torture people. A Boggart can be overcome by thinking about it looking idiotic, and shouting '*Riddikulus*'. The characters have a range of fears. For example, Ron Weasley is scared of spiders; Remus Lupin, of the full moon, as he fears turning into a werewolf. Hermione Granger has aspirational fears: she is terrified of Professor McGonagall telling her she has 'failed everything', as she is afraid of exam failure. Molly Weasley fears for others: she is panicked by the idea of seeing members of her family dead. For Harry it is Dementors, in whose presence he hears his mother's dying screams and who would suck out all his hope and happiness. The point is that if you run away from your fears they will remain bottled up and able to frighten you repeatedly when you are at your most vulnerable. If you face up to them, name them and ridicule or at least rationalise them, they will lose their power and may no longer blight your life. This is so, whether the fear is what others might deem to be irrational (I have a fear of sharks if I am alone in a swimming pool – maybe too much Jacques Cousteau at an impressionable age), or rational (Molly's family *was* in mortal danger).

Harry's chief fear is a combination of desolation, depression and abandonment, as epitomised by Dementors. In Gethsemane Jesus wrestles with the prospect of imminent flogging, crucifixion, abandonment by his friends and spiritual isolation. 'My God, my God, why have you forsaken me?'[77] So 'Jesus withdrew from his disciples about a stone's throw, knelt down, and prayed, "Father, if you are willing, remove this cup from me; yet, not my will but yours be done."'[78]

Perils of the press

Rowling offers a devastating critique of the tabloid press, with the reports which appear about Harry from the poisonous pen of journalist Rita Skeeter writing for the *Daily Prophet*. Rita has a magical nib called a Quick-Quotes Quill, which takes Harry's considered utterances and turns them into populist journalese. Rita manipulates Harry's interviews to make them more mawkishly marketable. This make him unpopular at school, as his fellow pupils assume that what they read in the newspaper is true, and that Harry is a boastful attention-seeker.

Matters deteriorate as the Ministry of Magic seeks to suppress news of the return of Voldemort and so takes control of the *Daily Prophet,* censoring its output. The reader is aware of the true situation and of the paper's distortion and suppression of the facts. A good insight for children to learn early on. Finally Hermione manages to blackmail Skeeter into publishing an accurate report to be published in Xenophilius[79] Lovegood's wacky but honest journal, *The Quibbler*. After Dumbledore's death, Rita Skeeter rushes out a dirt-dishing biography of him, using rumour, innuendo and some of Dumbledore's youthful indiscretions, as well as a twisted version of certain events in order to rubbish his reputation. Reading it shakes Harry, as his memories of Dumbledore as a wise, benevolent, protective father-figure are undermined. Is Dumbledore yet another adult in whom Harry has put his trust, and to an extent hero-worshipped, whose integrity is now suspect? This, after Harry had learned that both his father and his godfather, Sirius, were not as unswervingly heroic as he had at first thought. Developing a more realistic appraisal of his heroes is part of Harry's emotional maturing. However, the falsehoods published go too far.

Hopefully, this will give children a healthy scepticism about what they read in celebrity biography, magazines, blogs, tweets and newspapers. It might also help them recognise the value of a free press and how competition aids it.

3

Christian Values, Imagery and Biblical Quotes

Values

Core Christian values are manifest throughout the Harry Potter novels, most notably self-sacrificial love which defeats evil. We initially meet this in the first book[80] when we learn that Harry's mother put herself in the way of Voldemort's spell to kill her infant son, which saved him, and also in the dénouement of the last book, where Harry is himself prepared to die in order to defeat Lord Voldemort.

Forgiveness is demonstrated throughout the books. Harry does not take revenge on the frightful Dursleys who brought him up so neglectfully and abusively. He could have just left them to their fate at the hands of Voldemort's Death Eaters when he left home at seventeen, but he persuaded them to accept an escape plan. Harry, after years of being bullied by Draco Malfoy, could have killed him during fighting within Hogwarts School or allowed others to do so, but he didn't.

A powerful Christian message is given by the route of 'remorse', which Rowling offers to those who wish to turn from following the Dark Lord. This is about as close as one can get, without using specific Christian terminology, to Christ's call to 'repentance', turning away from spiritual darkness to the light, from evil to goodness, *metanoia*.[81]

For God so loved the world that he gave his only Son, so that everyone who believes in him may not perish but may have eternal life. Indeed, God did not send the Son into the world to condemn the world, but in order that the world might be saved through him. . . . And this is the judgment, that the light has come into the world, and people loved darkness rather than light because their deeds were evil. For all who do evil hate the light and do not come to the light, so that their deeds may not be exposed. But those who do what is true come to the light, so that it may be clearly seen that their deeds have been done in God.[82]

The theme of light and darkness, good and evil, runs through all the Harry Potter books, much as it does through John's Gospel.

Spiritual warfare is also a powerful theme throughout the books. Voldemort and his Dark Marked Death Eaters are like the cosmic powers and principalities mentioned by Paul, ranged against members of the Order of the Phoenix, those supporting justice, freedom and truth. Harry and his friends, in exercising Defence Against the Dark Arts, engage with the equivalent of the Pauline exhortation to:

Put on the whole armour of God, so that you may be able to stand against the wiles of the devil. For our struggle is not against enemies of blood and flesh, but against the rulers, against the authorities, against the cosmic powers of this present darkness, against the spiritual forces of evil in the heavenly places. Therefore take up the whole armour of God, so that you may be able to withstand on that evil day, and having done everything, to stand firm.[83]

Imagery

The phoenix

The phoenix has been a symbol of resurrection and renewed life for thousands of years. Herodotus, writing in c. 450 bc, described the phoenix as the symbolic bird of the city Heliopolis (city of the sun) which incinerates itself every 1,500 years and is then reborn. In Ancient Egypt it was known at the *boine* bird, the soul of the sun god, a name which somehow turned into phoenix. 'The Order of the Phoenix' is a group of wizards fighting against Voldemort. His symbol is a 'Dark Mark' etched on his followers' forearms. Dumbledore's pet is a phoenix named Fawkes.[84] He comes to the aid of Harry as he displays loyalty to Dumbledore when confronted by a deadly Basilisk and Voldemort.[85] The wands of both Harry and Voldemort each contain a tail feather from Fawkes and have mystically entangled properties.

The unicorn

When Voldemort is just beginning to regain a body he kills a unicorn and drinks its blood in order to become more corporeal. Within medieval literature and in depictions on tapestries, the unicorn is an image of purity. The hunting, killing and dying of a unicorn symbolises the passion of Christ. So Voldemort is violating a Christian image.

Crucifixion

There is a striking Christian reference in one of the most powerful and 'unforgivable' curses within the magical world. The *Cruciatus* curse causes intense pain throughout the body, incapacitating its victim, but leaving no physical trace. The word derives from the Latin for a cross and the verb to torture. Any Christian will recognise the allusion to crucifixion, the means by which Jesus was executed by the Romans. That mode of death was so painful and long-drawn out – as a warning to others – that the Romans eventually banned it in the late fourth century AD. Many of Rowling's other spells use delightful adaptations of Latin.

Blood sacrifice

Harry and Voldemort are inextricably linked by the shred of Voldemort's soul that became embedded in Harry when Voldemort attempted to kill him as an infant and later, when Voldemort takes Harry's blood in order to become corporeal. That blood contained the protection of Lily's self-sacrifice, protecting Harry and Voldemort. When Harry offers himself up to Voldemort to die, he remains protected.

In the Old Testament, the blood of animals had to be shed to obtain forgiveness for sins. Blood was associated with the life of the animal and could not be consumed. Jesus acted once for all as the perfect sacrifice for sin, as he had never sinned but took all the sins of the world upon him as he was flogged and, bleeding, was crucified. He died, giving his life as a ransom for many. At the Last Supper he gave his disciples bread and wine which he said were to be as his body and blood. Eating and drinking these in remembrance of him would spiritually fill them with his life. A shockingly powerful symbolic and spiritual act, which the Church has carried on down the ages.

The Eye of Providence

The symbol of the three Deathly Hallows is an equilateral triangle enclosing a circle with a vertical line down the centre. In the book it represents the Wand of Destiny and the Resurrection Stone enclosed by the Invisibility Cloak. I suspect the design was influenced by the Christian symbol of the Eye of Providence, the Eye of God, encased in an equilateral triangle which symbolised the Holy Trinity. An earlier depiction of this idea appeared on Egyptian pyramids dating from c. 2000 BC, some of which had a large eye painted on them. A version of this symbol was taken up by the Freemasons and also appears on US dollar bills. What the Deathly Hallows resembles is the eye not of a person, but that of a snake, which has a vertical slit as a pupil. Voldemort, we are first told, has 'livid scarlet eyes, and a nose that was flat as a snake's, with slits for nostrils.'[86] Later he is described as follows, 'his face shone through the gloom, hairless, snake-like, with slits for nostrils and gleaming red eyes whose pupils were vertical.'[87]

The drawings shown overleaf show, clockwise from top left:

- the eye of Horus, the falcon god, son of Isis and Osiris in Egyptian mythology, which dates back over 4000 years and which was painted on some pyramids

- the Christian icon of the Eye of Providence emphasizing the triangle as a symbol of the Holy Trinity, which is found in English and Greek churches

- a snake's head

- the sign of the Deathly Hallows, which symbolically represents all three objects: the vertical line is the Wand of Destiny, the circle is the Resurrection Stone, encased in an equilateral triangle, representing the Invisibility Cloak

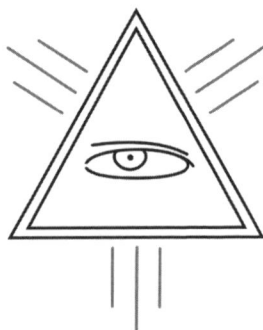

Christmas

One incongruous element of the wizarding world is that it celebrates Christmas. Hogwarts' hall is bedecked with decorations and houses numerous Christmas trees (which come from our pagan past), presents are exchanged and carols are sung. The children mostly go home for the Christmas holidays. Given how we in the UK celebrate Christmas, even though only about 1.5 million of whatever denomination regularly go to church, perhaps it is not that strange. The last survey suggested that some 70% of the UK's population called themselves Christians.[88] The tendency of local authorities to suppress the term 'Christmas' in favour of 'Wintervall' or some such title, coupled with shopping centres' habits of playing seasonal songs as long as no mention of the baby Jesus is made, just in case someone is offended, may move us into Hogwarts mode shortly, where we celebrate something that has no concept of God involved.[89]

Apocalypse

The calamitous events which lead up to the Battle of Hogwarts in the final book have parallels with biblical warnings of the showdown to come between the forces of good and evil here on earth. In Harry Potter's universe there are killings, disappearances and seemingly natural disasters. The humans, including the British Prime Minister, have to have wizard protectors, mostly unbeknown to them, to militate against the forces of destruction which Voldemort is unleashing upon the Muggle world. Then Voldemort launches his full forces onto Hogwarts. The staff, pupils and associated creatures fight back in what is an epic battle. Harry is 'the chosen one': the only person who can defeat Voldemort, as each contains a part of the other. Harry has to be prepared to be killed by Voldemort as the only way to defeat him. Finally, when Voldemort attempts to use the Wand of Destiny to kill Harry, it recognises its true master, the spell backfires and Voldemort is destroyed.

Jesus prophesied:

> And you will hear of wars and rumours of wars; see that you are not alarmed; for this must take place, but the end is not yet. For nation will rise against nation, and kingdom against kingdom, and there will be famines and earthquakes in various places: all this is but the beginning of the birth pangs.[90]

Following which we get in Revelation:

> And war broke out in heaven; Michael and his angels fought against

the dragon. The dragon and his angels fought back, but they were defeated, and there was no longer any place for them in heaven. The great dragon was thrown down, that ancient serpent, who is called the Devil and Satan, the deceiver of the whole world – he was thrown down to the earth, and his angels were thrown down with him.[91]

Finally, as prophesied in Daniel[92] and reiterated by Jesus, he himself will return in glory:

> Then the High Priest said to him, 'I put you under oath before the living God, tell us if you are the Messiah, the Son of God.' Jesus said to him, 'You have said so. But I tell you, From now on you will see the Son of Man seated at the right hand of Power and coming on the clouds of heaven.'[93]

Biblical quotes

In the churchyard in Godric's Hollow, where Harry's parents are buried, the carvings on two gravestones contain biblical quotations.[94] On that of Dumbledore's mother and sister it reads, 'Where your treasure is there will your heart be also', which comes from the Gospels. Jesus said:

> Lay not up for yourselves treasures upon earth, where moth and rust doth corrupt, and where thieves break through and steal: But lay up for yourselves treasures in heaven, where neither moth nor rust doth corrupt, and where thieves do not break through nor steal: For where your treasure is, there will your heart be also.[95]

On Harry's parents' gravestone is, 'The last enemy that shall be destroyed is death.' This is a quote from Paul's first letter to the Corinthians:

For as in Adam all die, even so in Christ shall all be made alive. But every man in his own order: Christ the firstfruits; afterward they that are Christ's at his coming. Then cometh the end, when he shall have delivered up the kingdom to God, even the Father; when he shall have put down all rule and all authority and power. For he must reign, till he hath put all enemies under his feet. The last enemy that shall be destroyed is death.[96]

For Christians death is not the end. In the words of the writer of Revelation:

Then I saw a new heaven and a new earth; for the first heaven and the first earth had passed away, and the sea was no more . . . And I heard a loud voice from the throne saying:

'See, the home of God is among mortals.
he will dwell with them as their God;
they will be his peoples,
and God himself will be with them;
he will wipe every tear from their eyes.
Death will be no more;
mourning and crying and pain will be no more,
for the first things have passed away.'[97]

In the Harry Potter universe death is not the end either. Harry meeting the dead Dumbledore and his hearing voices beyond the veil attest to that. Individuals brought back by the Resurrection Stone can interact with living people, but can never fully rejoin the living.

What the Bible says about magic

There is a handful of biblical verses referring to the practice of divination and sorcery and of those seeking to contact the dead. Basically it is forbidden in Leviticus:

> You shall not practice augury or witchcraft . . . Do not turn to mediums or wizards; do not seek them out, to be defiled by them: I am the Lord your God.'[98] and 'If any turn to mediums and wizards, prostituting themselves to them, I will set my face against them, and will cut them off from the people . . . A man or a woman who is a medium or a wizard shall be put to death; they shall be stoned to death, their blood is upon them.

The context of these commands includes the following, about which Christians seem less exercised these days:

> You shall not round off the hair on your temples or mar the edges of your beard. You shall not make any tattoo marks upon you: You shall not sow your field with two kinds of seed, [now thought to be ecologically sound]; nor shall you put on a garment made of two different materials [for example, poly-cotton shirts or silk-cashmere pashminas]. If a man commits adultery with the wife of his neighbour, both the adulterer and the adulteress shall be put to death.[99]

When King Saul, who had forbidden attempts to contact the dead and had driven out mediums from his land was in trouble, and could get no answer from God, he disguised himself and sought out the Witch of Endor, asking her to raise the shade of the prophet Samuel.[100] Samuel appears, angry that he has been summoned, and explains that God has removed his blessing and protection from Saul because of his disobedience. It is not that spiritualism never works, it is just that you don't know with what you might be dealing, whether with good spirits or with evil ones who might deceive you, and so you just shouldn't go there.

There is a meeting of magic and miracle in Exodus, when Moses goes to ask Pharaoh if the Israelites may leave:

> Moses and Aaron went to Pharaoh and did as the Lord had commanded; Aaron threw down his staff before Pharaoh and his officials, and it became a snake. Then Pharaoh summoned the wise men and the sorcerers; and they also, the magicians of Egypt, did the same by their secret arts. Each one threw down his staff, and they became snakes; but Aaron's staff swallowed up theirs.[101]

There are Ancient Egyptian figurines holding rigid snakes. This skill was seemingly passed down the millennia, as it was recorded by Edward Lane at the beginning of the nineteenth century.[102] So here we appear to have the miraculous – presumably Aaron didn't know how to do this on his own – beating the merely magical.

In the New Testament there are two instances of magicians being thwarted. Simon Magus offers Peter money to have the power of filling people with the Holy Spirit. Peter's reaction is:

> May your silver perish with you, because you thought you could obtain God's gift with money! You have no part or share in this, for your heart is not right before God. Repent therefore of this wickedness of yours, and pray to the Lord that, if possible, the intent of your heart may be forgiven you. For I see that you are in the gall of bitterness and the chains of wickedness.' Simon answered, 'Pray for me to the Lord, that nothing of what you have said may happen to me.[103]

The other occasion was when a slave girl who told fortunes was trailing after Paul and crying out, 'These men are slaves of the Most High God, who proclaim to you a way of salvation.' He became so irritated that he said to the divining spirit within her, 'I order you in the name of Jesus Christ to come out of her.'[104] And it did. Her owners who made money from her divination were furious. This resulted in Paul and Silas getting beaten and put into prison for 'breaching the peace'.

In Revelation, Chapters 21 and 22, sorcerers are condemned, along with the cowardly, faithless, the polluted, murderers, fornicators, idolaters and all liars. However, Jesus offers forgiveness for our sins. Otherwise, the vast majority of the world's population would end up in one of these categories, if not by their actions then by their thoughts. As Jesus pointed out in the Sermon on the Mount, looking lustfully at someone [and fantasising about it] is committing adultery in your heart.

Divination in Harry Potter

Divination at Hogwarts is the type of magic taken least seriously. In fact the teacher, Sybil Trelawney, and the subject, are generally considered to be rather fraudulent and few students pay attention. There are a couple of prophecies regarding Harry which are realised but the most crucial one is only enacted because Voldemort believes it and effectively makes his own worst fears come true. This was during Trelawney's job interview for a Hogwarts teaching post, when she entered a trance and prophesied the time of birth of a wizard who would have the power to vanquish Voldemort. Half of it is overheard by Snape who repeats it to Voldemort, prompting him to attempt to kill the infant Harry.[105]

This is similar to the situation described by Shakespeare in the encounter Macbeth has with the three witches who greet him:

> 'All hail Macbeth, hail to thee Thane of Glamis.'
> 'All hail Macbeth, hail to thee Thane of Cawdor.'
> 'All hail Macbeth, that shall be King hereafter.'

Macbeth is already Thane of Glamis and is made Thane of Cawdor shortly after that prophesy, by King Duncan. It is this which prompts Macbeth, encouraged by his wife, to murder Duncan and seize the crown. This would probably never have occurred to him, without hearing and being tempted by the witches' prophecy.

Consider a biblical parallel:

In the time of King Herod, after Jesus was born in Bethlehem of Judea, wise men from the East came to Jerusalem, asking, "Where is the child who has been born king of the Jews? For we observed his star at its rising, and have come to pay him homage." When King Herod heard this, he was frightened, and all Jerusalem with him; and calling together all the chief priests and scribes of the people, he inquired of them where the Messiah was to be born. They told him, "In Bethlehem of Judea; for so it has been written by the prophet: [Micah 5:2] And you, Bethlehem, in the land of Judah, are by no means least among the rulers of Judah; for from you shall come a ruler who is to shepherd my people Israel." Then Herod secretly called for the wise men and learned from them the exact time when the star had appeared. Then he sent them to Bethlehem, saying, "Go and search diligently for the child; and when you have found him, bring me word so that I may also go and pay him homage." When they had heard the king, they set out; and there, ahead of them, went the star that they had seen at its rising, until it stopped over the place where the child was. When they saw that the star had stopped, they were overwhelmed with joy. On entering the house, they saw the child with Mary his mother; and they knelt down and paid him homage. Then, opening their treasure chests, they offered him gifts of gold, frankincense, and myrrh. And having been warned in a dream not to return to Herod, they left for their own country by another road . . . When Herod saw that he had been tricked by the wise men, he was infuriated, and he sent orders to kill all the boys in and around Bethlehem who were two years old or under.[106]

Other magic in Harry Potter

Much of the magic used by the wizarding world is a mirror of human beings' development of technology. Arthur Weasley, Ron's father, is fascinated by technology and by describing it in the way she does, Rowling gets us to think through many of the engineering developments humans have achieved, for example in transport, communications, power generation, building, household machines and food preparation. Magic is also employed as armaments and for defence, in order to heal, to decorate homes and for many other uses. As with our technology, it can be used for good or ill.

In Harry Potter, magic seems at times to have a will of its own. The wand chooses the wizard. When young witches and wizards are taken to obtain their first wand, the wand-maker may offer one he thinks will suit the individual but it is the wand that chooses its owner. A witch or wizard can use another's wand but it will not work so well for them unless they have defeated its previous owner, and so won the allegiance of the wand. This is demonstrated when Voldemort uses Lucius Malfoy's and then Dumbledore's Wand of Destiny, thinking they can defeat Harry's.[107] The fact that Harry and Voldemort's original wands both contained a tail feather from Fawkes the phoenix may be part of the reason why they appear to have entangled properties.

In the Bible there are repeated examples of the fact that it is God who first calls us. For example:

Adam and Eve heard the sound of the Lord God walking in the garden at the time of the evening breeze, and the man and his wife hid themselves from the presence of the Lord God among the trees of the garden. But the Lord God called to the man, and said to him, 'Where are you?'[108]

O Lord, you have searched me and known me. You know when I sit down and when I rise up; you discern my thoughts from far away . . . For it was you who formed my inward parts; you knit me together in my mother's womb . . . My frame was not hidden from you, when I was being made in secret, intricately woven in the depths of the earth. Your eyes beheld my unformed substance. In your book were written all the days that were formed for me, when none of them as yet existed.[109]

Jesus said to his disciples, 'You did not choose me but I chose you. And I appointed you to go and bear fruit, fruit that will last, so that the Father will give you whatever you ask him in my name.'[110]

We know that all things work together for good for those who love God, who are called according to his purpose. For those whom he foreknew he also predestined to be conformed to the image of his Son, in order that he might be the firstborn within a large family. And those whom he predestined he also called; and those whom he called he also justified; and those whom he justified he also glorified.[111]

In Harry Potter there are three 'unforgivable curses': the Imperius, Cruciatus and Avada Kedavra. The Imperius name derives from the Latin meaning to command, commanding. It enables the curser to have complete body and mind control over the cursed, removing their free will and commanding them to act according to the will of the one who has cursed them. The Cruciatus curse, derived from the Latin for cross and to torture, causes indescribable pain and was used on Neville Longbottom's parents to drive them mad. It leaves no physical trace. Avada Kedavra is a killing curse (presumably derived from the traditional words of the magic spell Abracadabra).[112] In the Bible Jesus says that the only unforgivable sin is to blaspheme against the Holy Spirit.[113] He doesn't define what that is and consequently the idea has exercised theologians over the centuries. It may be the final turning away from God, refusing to negotiate or admit wrongdoing, resulting in being cast down with Lucifer, forever banished from the divine presence.

Will Harry Potter entice children to dabble in the occult?

Rowling has been asked about whether she thinks Harry Potter could attract children to the occult. On her website she states that although she has spoken to many children about her books over the years, none of them has ever claimed a desire to engage in witchcraft. Her detractors might quote Mandy Rice-Davies during the John Profumo call-girl trial, 'Well, she would say that, wouldn't she?' However, given that in the Harry Potter world one cannot become a witch or wizard, but is *born* one, with varying levels of talent, children reading the books, who tend to think more literally than some adults, are unlikely to consider that they could become magical by trying. In Harry Potter's world one may be born with the talent but it is clear that education and training are required to hone and control it, hence the need for Hogwarts and the other wizarding schools. At Hogwarts there are strict moral guidelines that the powers should only be used for good, although students should learn Defence Against the Dark Arts, as there are some who will use magical powers for evil intent.

Conclusion

The world view depicted by Rowling in the Harry Potter series is highly moral and in many ways congruent with the Judeo-Christian tradition. It is of course also radically different from ours in some important respects. Clearly our world does not have a group of people with magical powers that the witches and wizards possess. There is another crucial difference between our world and that of Harry Potter. Any human being may become a Christian. It only requires a step of faith, a preparedness to engage with God through Jesus Christ and submit to his will. In Harry Potter's world you either have magical powers or you don't; you cannot become a witch or wizard by trying. This is an important distinction when it comes to assessing whether the books would lead children into engaging with the occult, which I do not believe they would.

Rowling explores a range of issues which have their biblical parallels as well as being important current social concerns. These encompass: authority, its source and the exercise thereof; anti-racism; gender equality; slavery; bullying; the vagaries of the press; and the abuse of power. The themes of death, bereavement and the afterlife run through all the books. There is no underage drinking of alcohol, no recreational drugs are taken and sexual activity is not mentioned overtly, but its ideal within the married state is implied. Good school discipline and a work ethic, with healthy competition are all promoted. Qualities like loyalty, friendship,

forgiveness, courage and compassion are valued. Rowling emphasises the idea that the person you are is demonstrated by the choices
you make, more than by your parentage and upbringing. Or as Jesus
said, 'You will know them by their fruits.'[114] Most of all, Rowling
emphasises the redeeming power of love.

Rowling employs Christian imagery, and the route to turning
from following evil to working for the common good is 'remorse';
repentance by any other name. Harry can only finally defeat the
power of evil by himself being prepared to die. Most of the witchcraft replaces our technological developments. Divination, the
summoning up of spirits of the dead, which is forbidden in the
Bible, is played down in Harry Potter's world.

J.K. Rowling was brought up an Anglican and is now a member
of the Church of Scotland. She is quoted as saying, 'To me, the
religious parallels have always been obvious . . . but I never wanted
to talk too openly about it because I thought it might show people
who just wanted the story, where we were going . . . I think those
two particular [biblical] quotations he [Harry] finds on the tombstones, they sum up, they almost epitomise, the whole series.' These
are, 'Where your treasure is, there will your heart be also.' and 'The
last enemy that shall be destroyed is death.'[115]

Glossary

Avada Kedavra: a killing curse, (presumably derived from the traditional words of the magic spell Abracadabra). Abracadabra was first found in literature in 1696 and is associated with Roman period cabalistic charms containing the Greek ABRAXAS, *The Shorter Oxford English Dictionary.*

blood traitor: a pure-blood witch or wizard who consorts with Mudbloods.

Boggart: a shape-shifting creature which assumes the appearance of your worst fears. It can be mastered by imagining it looking idiotic, and shouting '*Ridikulus*' at it.

butterbeer: a drink containing negligible amounts of alcohol.

Cruciatus curse: causes intense pain throughout the body incapacitating its victim, but leaving no physical trace. The word derives from the Latin for a cross and to torture – hence crucifixion.

Daily Prophet: the official wizarding newspaper. Once the Ministry of Magic attempts to suppress the news that Voldemort has returned, it influences the paper's output.

Dark Mark: a brand on the forearms of followers of Lord Voldemort.

Death Eater: a follower of Lord Voldemort who has a Dark Mark branded on their forearm.

Deathly Hallows: the symbol of the three Deathly Hallows is an equilateral triangle enclosing a circle with a vertical line down the centre. In the books it represents the Wand of Destiny and the Resurrection Stone enclosed by the Invisibility Cloak. Three charmed items which together would give their owner immense power and an ability to control the world.

Defence Against the Dark Arts: school subject in which students learn how to counter dark magic.

Dementor: a creature which sucks all the joy out of people so they think they can never be happy again. At worst, one can kiss you and suck out your soul, leaving you a living husk.

half-blood: a witch or wizard with one non-magical or Muggle parent and one wizarding parent.

Horcruxes: objects in which Lord Voldemort has hidden shards of his soul in order to attempt to remain immortal. They include a diary, the Resurrection Stone in a ring, the Slytherin locket, the Hufflepuff cup, the Ravenclaw diadem, the snake Nagini and, unintentionally, in Harry Potter.

house-elf: a creature with big bat-like ears and huge bulging eyes, able to perform particular types of magic. They are effectively slaves, often owned by ancient wizarding families and can only be freed by being given items of clothing to wear by their masters. The cooking and cleaning at Hogwarts is done by elves. Hermione tries to free them but not all elves, let alone wizards, are enthusiastic about the idea.

Imperius curse: the Imperius name derives from the Latin meaning to command or commanding. It enables the curser to have complete body and mind control over the cursed, removing their free will and commanding them to act according to the will of the one who has cursed them.

Inferi: corpses whose bodies can be taken over and controlled by Dark Magic, rather like horror movie zombies.

Mirror of Erised: a mirror which shows you your deepest desire

– Erised is desire spelled backwards – not quite mirror writing, as the letters are the correct way round.

Mudblood: a witch or wizard whose parents are normal human beings lacking magical gifts, i.e. Muggles.

Muggle: a normal human beings lacking magical gifts.

Order of the Phoenix: an organisation dedicated to defeating Lord Voldemort.

Portkey: an ordinary object bewitched to transport anyone touching it to a predetermined location at a set time.

pure-blood: a witch or wizard both of whose parents were magical and who may trace their family back through pure wizarding blood lines.

Quidditch: the school sport played flying on broomsticks involving bats, balls, goals and a tiny flying ball, called the Snitch, which, if caught, finishes the game and scores high points. It is played on equal terms by boys and girls.

Squib: the offspring of wizarding parents who, humiliatingly, themselves lack any magical powers.

Triwizard Tournament: a competition held at Hogwarts between representatives of three schools of witchcraft and wizarding: Hogwarts in the UK, Beauxbatons from France and Durmsdrang from north-eastern Europe.

Notes

1 Jonathan Petre, Religion Correspondent, www.telegraph.co.uk, 20 October 2007.

2 Matthew 6:21, Luke 12:34, 1 Corinthians 15:26, *King James* translation.

3 BBC Online 12 December 2001.

4 *Harry Potter and the Sorcerer's Stone* in USA editions.

5 Mark 3:21.

6 Luke 6:27.

7 Mark 14:36.

8 Sirius is the name of what is known as the 'dog star' and his animagus, the animal shape he can assume, is that of a dog. His elder brother was called Regulus Arcturus. Regulus is the name of a star in the constellation Leo and Arcturus, in Boötes. Their father was called Orion and they have a cousin, Bellatrix, meaning a female warrior, which is also the name of the star – the western shoulder of the constellation of Orion. The family sport several other astronomical names. All part of Rowling's erudition and fun.

9 *Harry Potter and the Deathly Hallows* Ch. 18.

10 Matthew 26:39b–40.

11 *Harry Potter and the Deathly Hallows* Ch.35.

12 Matthew 15:24f.

13 John 11:21–3.

14 John 19:26–7.

15 *Harry Potter and the Philosopher's Stone* Ch.16.

16 Plato in the *Republic* says that a good constitution is only possible when the ruler does not want to rule; where men contend for power, where they have not learned to distinguish between the art of getting hold of the helm of state and the art of steering, which alone is statesmanship, true politics is impossible. *A Treatise on Government*, translated from the Greek of Aristotle by William Ellis, London &Toronto, J.M.Dent & Sons Ltd. First issue of this edition 1912. Reviewer D. Lindsay.

17 *Harry Potter and the Deathly Hallows* Ch.35.

18 *Harry Potter and the the Half-Blood Prince* Ch.26.

19 Who becomes Lord Voldemort.

20 Exodus 3:2, 13:21, Genesis 15:17, 1 Kings 18:38 and also Daniel 7:9–10

21 Matthew 7:13.

22 Acts 15:38–40.

23 'I say nothing about your owing me even your own self.' Philemon 1:19b So, why mention the debt if it is not being used to coerce Philemon?

24 1 Corinthians 9:22b.

25 Philippians 1:21.

26 Isaiah 14:12–15.

27 Luke 10:18–19.

28 Genesis 3:8–24.

29 Book 1 lines 84–7.

30 Rowling may have derived Nagini's name from the *Naja naja*, or Indian Cobra, which features in Indian mythology, whose name derives from the Sanskrit *Naag*.

31 His name is an anagram of 'I am Lord Voldemort' – *Harry Potter and the Chamber of Secrets* Ch.17.

32 www.hare.org.

33 Hare, Robert D. *Without Conscience: The Disturbing World of Psychopaths Among Us*, New York, Pocket Books, 1993, p. 2.

34 Exodus 3:14.

35 John 1:12 ὅσοι δὲ ἔλαβον αὐτόν, ἔδωκεν αὐτοῖς ἐξουσίαν τέκνα θεοῦ γενέσθαι, τοῖς πιστεύουσιν εἰς τὸ ὄνομα αὐτοῦ.

36 Mark 15:39.

37 Ps 90:4 For a thousand years in your sight are like yesterday. Note: God's day lengths are not ours!

38 Genesis 1:1-2:1.

39 It may also be no accident that Rowling wrote the Harry Potter saga in seven books.

40 The diary, Resurrection Stone in the ring, Slytherin locket, Hufflepuff cup, Ravenclaw diadem, snake Nagini, unintentionally in Harry and, presumably, a bit left over in his disembodied self.

41 'Praise my soul the King of Heaven', H.F. Lyte based on Ps. 103.

42 *Harry Potter and the Deathly Hallows* Ch.35.

43 Revelation 14:9b–11.

44 *Harry Potter and the Order of the Phoenix* Ch.9.

45 John 11:50.

46 *Harry Potter and the Goblet of Fire* Ch.32 and *Harry Potter and the Deathly Hallows* Ch.23.

47 Matthew 27:4–5.

48 Galatians 3:28.

49 'Dolores' means pain and she causes Harry much pain by having him write the line 'I must not tell lies' which is incised on the back of his hand each time he does it. He had just declared that Voldemort had returned and that he had fought him.

50 Dementors are creatures who suck all the joy out of people so they think they can never be happy again. At worst they can suck out your soul.

51 *Harry Potter and the Order of the Phoenix* Ch.8.

52 Matthew 9:5–7.

53 Matthew 12:27.

54 Mark 11:30, Matthew 21:25 & Luke 20:4.

55 *Critical Perspectives on Harry Potter*, ed. Elizabeth E. Heilman, 2nd edn 2009, London, Routledge.

56   *Harry Potter and the Half-Blood Prince* Ch. 26.

57   *Harry Potter and the Order of the Phoenix* Ch. 35.

58   Mark 15:38.

59   Romans 10:9.

60   1 Corinthians 2:9.

61   Romans 8:37-9.

62   *Harry Potter and the Deathly Hallows* Ch.35.

63   2 Corinthians 12:1b–4.

64   Matthew 16:25, also similar in Mark 8:35, Luke 9:24 and John 12:25.

65   'The creed which accepts as the foundation of morals, Utility, or the Greatest Happiness Principle, holds that actions are right in proportion as they tend to promote happiness, wrong as they tend to produce the reverse of happiness. By happiness is intended pleasure, and the absence of pain; by unhappiness, pain, and the privation of pleasure.' *Utilitarianism*, John Stuart Mill (1863), Chapter 2.

66   *Harry Potter and the Deathly Hallows* Ch.18.

67   Philippians 3:4b–6.

68   Deuteronomy 21:18–20.

69   Luke 2:48–50.

70   Luke 10:38.

71   20th October 2007.

72   Matthew 3:8–10; 7:15-20, Luke 3:9, 6:43–5, John 15:2f.

73   *Harry Potter and the Philosopher's Stone* Ch.7.

74   Matthew 7:13–14.

75   She is a frightening example of the phrase, the *banality of evil* coined by Hannah Arendt and incorporated in the title of her 1963 work, *Eichmann in Jerusalem: A Report on the Banality of Evil.* It describes the thesis that the great evils in history in general, and the Holocaust in particular, were not executed by fanatics or sociopaths but rather by ordinary people who accepted the premises of their state and therefore participated with the view that their actions were normal.

76   Song written and performed by Carly Simon, 1972.

77 Mark 15:34, Matthew 27:46.

78 Luke 22:42–4.

79 'Xenophilus' means 'lover of foreigners'.

80 *Harry Potter and the Philosopher's Stone.*

81 *Metanoia* afterthought, change of mind, repentance.

82 John 3:16–21.

83 Ephesians 6:12f.

84 Nice touch, as Guy Fawkes attempted to incinerate the Houses of Parliament in the Gunpowder Plot of 1605, the thwarting of which we celebrate on 5 November.

85 *Harry Potter and the Chamber of Secrets* Ch.17.

86 *Harry Potter and the Goblet of Fire* Ch.32.

87 *Harry Potter and the Deathly Hallows* Ch.1.

88 Office of National Statistics, Integrated Household Survey, 2010.

89 Ironically, I entered a large hotel in Amman, Jordan, a mainly Muslim country, on the 6 December 2010, and the lobby music was back-to-back Christmas carols!

90 Matthew 24:6–8.

91 Revelation 12:7–9.

92 Daniel 7:13.

93 Matthew 26:63

94 *Harry Potter and the Deathly Hallows* Ch. 16.

95 Matthew 6:19–21, also Luke 12:34, *King James* translation.

96 1 Corinthians 15:22–26, *King James* translation.

97 Revelation 21:1–4.

98 Leviticus 19:26, 31 & 20:6,27.

99 Leviticus 19:19, 27–28; 20: 10.

100 1 Samuel 28:3–19.

101 Exodus 7:10–12

102 *Manners and Customs of the Modern Egyptians*, E.W. Lane, first published 1836.

103 Acts 8:20–24

104 Acts 16:17f.

105 *Harry Potter and the Order of the Phoenix* Ch. 37.

106 Matthew 2:1f. Part of Herod's paranoia was caused by the fact that he wasn't ethnically Jewish, but the son of a second-generation Idumean convert to Judaism and an Arab mother. No 'pure blood' there.

107 *Harry Potter and the Deathly Hallows.*

108 Genesis 3:8–9.

109 Ps.139:1–2,13,15–16.

110 John 15:16.

111 Romans 8:28–30.

112 Abracadabra was first found in literature in 1696 and is associated with Roman period cabalistic charms containing the Greek ABRAXAS, *The Shorter Oxford English Dictionary.*

113 Matthew 12:32.

114 Matthew 7:16.

115 Matthew 6:21 & Luke 12:34 and 1 Corinthians 15:26, *King James* translation.

Study Guide

The following table lists values or situations which occur in the Old and New Testaments, followed by examples of similar circumstances arising in the Harry Potter books. You may like to read the passages where relevant and then consider if you have ever had to face a similar situation in your own life.

- If so, what did you do or say? How did you feel about it? What was the outcome?

- Thinking about it again, would you react in the same way or differently? Why might that be?

- Can you imagine a circumstance where such a situation or required quality might occur in your life now?

- How do you think you might react? Would it be like people in Harry Potter or in the Bible or in a different way?

- What sort of example for our lives do you think the Harry Potter books set regarding this issue? Why? Is that a good way to react to such circumstances?

Abbreviations

CS *Harry Potter and the Chamber of Secrets*
DH *Harry Potter and the Deathly Hallows*
GF *Harry Potter and the Goblet of Fire*
H-BP *Harry Potter and the Half-blood Prince*
HP *Harry Potter*
NT *New Testament*
OP *Harry Potter and the Order of the Phoenix*
OT *Old Testament*
PA *Harry Potter and the Prisoner of Azkaban*
PS *Harry Potter and the Philosopher's Stone*

Value	Source	Example	Reference
Self-sacrificial love	OT	Abraham being prepared to sacrifice his son Isaac, even though he was the child of God's promise to give him decedents.	Genesis 22:1–14
	OT	Eli understanding Hannah's desire for a child, who would then be dedicated to the Lord.	1 Samuel 1:9–20
	NT	Mary's acceptance of the role God chose for her in being the mother of his son.	Luke 1: 26–38
	NT	Jesus' mission on earth, to take the sins of the world and atone for them, dying for us so that we may be reconciled to God.	Matthew 26:26–29, Mark 8:31
	HP	Harry's father James dies trying to protect his wife and child. His mother Lily offers her life when Voldemort is about to kill Harry.	PS Ch.4
	HP	Sirius fights and dies protecting Harry and his friends.	OP Ch.35
	HP	Harry is prepared to die to defeat Voldemort.	DH Ch.34
	HP	Remus Lupin, Tonks and Fred Weasley all die in the Battle of Hogwarts.	DH Ch.31
	HP	Severus Snape leads a double life, pretending to work for Voldemort while always protecting Harry, because he loved Harry's mother.	DH Ch.33
Friendship	OT	David and Jonathan.	1 Samuel 18:1–5, 19:1–7, 20:1–23

	NT	Jesus with Peter, John and James	Matthew 17:1–8, 26:36–46, Mark 1: 29–31, Luke 5: 1–11
	NT	Jesus with Martha, Mary and Lazarus	Luke 10:38–42, John 11: 1–44
	HP	Harry and Ron start up a friendship on the Hogwarts express train. After a sticky start, Hermione joins them.	PS Ch.6 & 10
	HP	Neville Longbottom tries to stop Harry, Ron and Hermione going out at night and getting into danger.	PS Ch.16
Fear	OT	Gideon's call by God to be a mighty warrior and defeat the Midianites.	Judges 6:11–24
	OT	Elijah flees from Queen Jezebel who is trying to kill him.	1 King 19:1–10
	OT	Jonah's call from God to warn Nineveh that if the citizens did not repent of their evil ways he would destroy them.	Jonah 1: 1–17
	NT	Peter's three-time denial of knowing Jesus after he had been arrested.	Matthew 26:69–75
	NT	Jesus praying in Gethsemane knowing that he was about to be arrested and killed.	Mark 14:32–42
	NT	The shepherds out in the fields when an angel appears to tell them of Jesus' birth.	Luke 2: 8–12
	NT	Women at Jesus' tomb.	Mark 16: 1–8

	HP	Harry's uncle Vernon attempts to flee the letters inviting Harry to Hogwarts School by escaping to a shack on a tiny island.	PS Ch.3
	HP	Voldemort's fear of death causing him to spilt his soul, hiding parts of it in Horcruxes.	H–BP Ch.23
	HP	Everyone's fear of Voldemort, whether supporters or opposers, such that they cannot even refer to him by name.	Various: starting in PS Ch.4
	HP	Others' fear of Harry's ability to talk to snakes.	CS Ch.11
	HP	Fear of Sirius Black who was thought to be a murderer with designs on Harry's life.	PA Ch.4 onwards
	HP	Boggarts, which are shape-shifters, assuming that image of which you are most frightened. They are combated by ridiculing them.	PA Ch.7
Courage	OT	Jacob wrestles with God.	Genesis 32:22–32
	OT	Moses confronting Pharaoh when asking for the Israelite slaves to be released to worship God.	Exodus 7:8-8:15
	OT	Moses stretching out his arm over the Red Sea to part the waves for the Israelites to cross over.	Exodus 14:21–29
	OT	David fighting the giant Philistine Goliath.	1 Samuel 17:21–50
	NT	Jesus fulfilling his destiny by journeying on to Jerusalem to certain betrayal, torture and death.	Matthew 16:21–23, 20:17–19
	NT	The women staying at the Cross when Jesus is crucified.	Mark 15:33–41

	HP	Ron playing wizards' chess which requires him to sacrifice himself.	PS Ch.16
	HP	Ron going into the forest following a trail of spiders even though he is frightened of spiders.	CS Ch.15
	HP	Harry fighting the Basilisk while trying to save Ginny.	CS Ch.17
	HP	Harry and Hermione entering the Whomping Willow when Ron is dragged into it.	PA Ch.17
	HP	Harry saving Gabrielle Delacour from apparent drowning in the Triwizard Tournament.	GF Ch.26
	HP	Harry entering The Department of Mysteries in the Ministry of Magic to save Sirius whom Harry thinks is being held there by Voldemort.	OP Chs. 34, 35
	HP	Snape acting as a double agent pretending to be loyal to Voldemort while protecting Harry.	DH Ch.33
Loyalty	OT	Joshua: 'As for me and my house we will serve the Lord.'	Joshua 24:14–28
	OT	Ruth and Naomi.	Ruth 1: 1–18
	NT	The women who stuck with Jesus through crucifixion and resurrection.	Mark 15:33–41 and Matthew 27:45–56
	NT	Friends of the paralytic who lowered him through the roof to Jesus' feet hoping that he would be cured.	Mark 2: 1–12
	NT	Roman centurion who asks Jesus to heal his slave who is dying.	Luke 7: 2–10

	HP	Hermione takes blame for the three of them being in the girls' lavatory with the troll.	PS Ch.10
	HP	When confronted by Riddle/Voldemort in the Chamber of Secrets, Harry announces that Dumbledore is the greatest wizard in the world (rather than Voldemort), so summoning help in the form of Dumbledore's pet phoenix Fawkes and the Gryffindor sword with which to kill the Basilisk.	CS Ch.17
	HP	Harry helps Cedric Digory in the Tri-wizard tournament and Cedric returns the favour.	GF Chs.20, 23
	HP	Snape is loyal to Dumbledore to the end, even though it doesn't look like it initially.	DH Ch.33
	HP	Ron and Hermione help Harry even when he has no idea what to do next.	DH Ch.19
Compassion	OT	Eli blessing Hannah who couldn't have children.	1 Samuel 1:9–20
	OT	Elijah and widow of Zarephath.	1 Kings 17:8–16
	NT	Jesus restoring the High Priest's slave's cut-off ear.	Luke 22:50–51
	NT	Jesus weeping for the dead Lazarus and his grieving family.	John 11:28–37
	NT	Jesus having compassion on the crowds following him and so teaching them and feeding them, rather than going off to get some rest.	Matthew 14:13–21

	HP	Ron and Harry going to find Hermione who doesn't know there is a troll on the loose, even though, at that stage, they can't stand her.	PS Ch.10
	HP	Hermione trying to free the house-elves, who effectively are wizards' slaves.	GF Ch. 21
	HP	Harry not allowing Remus Lupin and Sirius Black to kill Peter Pettigrew, having been unveiled as James and Lily's betrayer, when they had the chance.	PA Ch.19
Doing the right thing, rather than the easy one, even if the easy one is obeying the rules	OT	Rahab telling the citizens of Jericho that the Israelite spies had escaped when she was hiding them on her roof.	Joshua 2:1–14
	NT	Jesus healing people on the Sabbath.	Matthew 12:8–14, Luke 13:10–17
	HP	When Hermione is crying in the girls' lavatory and the troll is on the loose, Harry and Ron ignore instructions to go straight to their House and go and find her.	PS Ch.10
	HP	Harry, Ron and Hermione follow Quirrel onto the forbidden third-floor corridor where the three-headed dog is guarding a trapdoor.	PS Ch.16
	HP	Harry and Ron entering the girls' lavatory, as that contained the entrance to the Chamber of Secrets.	CS Ch.16

	HP	Protecting Sirius, who was a wanted criminal, from the Dementors.	PA Ch.21
	HP	Harry teaches 'Dumbledore's Army' Defence Against the Dark Arts when they are no longer being taught anything at Hogwarts.	OP Ch.18
Corruption	OT	God does not desire blood sacrifices but that people should do good and act justly.	Isaiah 1: 11–20 and Micah 6:8
	OT	Story of the false prophet.	1 Kings 13:11–25 (26-32)
	OT	Eli's sons stealing from the sacrificed meat offered to God.	1 Samuel 2:12–17
	NT	Jesus railing against the hypocrisy of the Pharisees.	Matthew 23: 1–36
	NT	Pontius Pilate agreeing to Jesus' crucifixion even though he could not convict him of a capital crime.	Matthew 27:11–26
	HP	Gilderoy Lockhart, the Defence Against the Dark Arts teacher, has built his entire career on appropriating other wizards' and witches' magical achievements and passing them off as his own. His one gift is erasing others' memories, enabling him to get away with it. This puts the school in danger.	CS. Ch.16
	HP	Harry in a rigged trial ordered by the Ministry of Magic when he had used magic to defend himself against Dementors.	OP Ch.8
	HP	Lucius Malfoy paying for Cornelius Fudge's pet projects thereby blinding him to Malfoy's loyalties to Voldemort.	OP Ch.9

Discipline, authorities and Hogwarts School	OT	The Ten Commandments and the golden rule	Exodus 20:1–17 and Leviticus 19:18
	NT	Paul writes that Christians should submit to the authorities. However he broke rules and took the punishment.	Romans 13:1–5, 2 Corinthians 11:21–25
	HP	Harry, Ron, Hermione and Draco are given detention for being out in Hagrid's hut after hours.	PS Ch.15
Resisting temptation	OT	Potiphar's wife attempting to seduce her husband's slave, Joseph.	Genesis 39:1–23
	NT	Jesus resisting the Devil in the wilderness.	Matthew 4:1–11
	NT	Peter trying to persuade Jesus not to go to Jerusalem and his death.	Matthew 16:21–23
	HP	Harry saving the Dursley family after the appalling way they have treated him.	DH Ch.3
	HP	The Mirror of Erised, showing you your greatest desire.	PS Ch. 12
	HP	Draco unable to kill Dumbledore.	H-BP Ch. 27
	HP	Harry refuses to leave Draco Malfoy to die in the Room of Requirement rescues him.	DH Ch. 31
Generosity	OT	God feeds the Israelites in the desert with manna and quails. Eventually he leads them into the Promised Land flowing with milk and honey.	Exodus 16:9–20 and Exodus 33:1–3
	NT	After the wine had run out, Jesus produces gallons more at the wedding feast in Cana.	John 2: 1–11

	NT	Jesus feeding 5,000 families from five loaves and two fishes.	Mark 6: 30–44
	HP	Harry shares sweets and chocolate on the Hogwarts Express with Ron, whom he has only just met.	PS Ch.6
	HP	Harry gives his winnings from the Triwizard Tournament to Fred and George Weasley to start up their joke shop.	GF Ch. 37
Anti-racism	OT	Two tribes are in a dispute. Members of one are identified by their inability to pronounce the word Shibboleth.	Judges 12:1–6
	NT	Jews and Gentiles before and after the New Covenant. Paul claims impeccable Jewish pedigree and now realises one is saved thought faith not blood line.	Philippians 3:1f
	HP	Ron defending Hermione when Draco calls her a Mudblood.	CS Ch.7
Combating injustice/ defence of the weak	OT	Nathan admonishing David for having Bathsheba's husband Uriah killed, after David had made her pregnant.	2 Samuel 11:1–12:15
	NT	Jesus' teaching.	Matthew 23:1–12, 23-26, Luke 18: 1–8
	NT	Care of Christian widows and the poor in Acts.	Acts 6:1-6
	NT	Jesus' trials with Sanhedrin and Pilate.	Matthew 26:57–68, 27:1–2, 11–26
	NT	Herod beheading John the Baptist.	Matthew 14:3–12

	HP	Harry flies his broomstick for the first time to catch a fragile 'Remembrall' that Draco had taken from Neville and tried to break.	PS Ch.9
	HP	Tom Riddle aged 13 (who becomes Lord Voldemort), frames the young Hagrid, claiming that Hagrid had opened the Chamber of Secrets, thereby getting Hagrid expelled from Hogwarts.	CS Ch.17
Dealing with fame/notoriety	OT	Women singing about and celebrating David's killing tens of thousands of his enemies whereas Saul is only recorded as killing thousands. This makes Saul jealous of David and he tries to kill him.	1 Samuel 18:6–11
	NT	Jesus's family coming to take him away as they are told he is mad.	Mark 3:19b–27
	NT	Jesus having to hide away from the crowds after feeding the 5,000 families, as they want to make him king.	John 6: (1–14), 15
	NT	Peter and John in Jerusalem proclaiming the Gospel.	Acts 4: 1–22
	HP	Gilderoy Lockhart revels in his self-publicity and plays it up. Harry cringes at his fame as 'the boy who lived' and tries to avoid having his photo taken by a star-struck pupil Colin Creevey.	CS Ch.6
Authority and accountability	NT	The Temple hierarchy challenging the source of Jesus' authority.	Matthew 21:23–27
	NT	Paul asserting his divine authority despite not having been a direct disciple of Jesus.	Galatians 1:11–24

	HP	With pupils terrified by the petrifaction of pupils and a cat, the Ministry of Magic and Hogwarts' governors feel the need to act without understanding the situation. Cornelius Fudge arrests Hagrid and removes him to prison and Dumbledore is suspended from his role as headmaster.	CS Ch.14
Persecution and abuse of power or position	OT	Eli's sons' behaviour regarding people's offerings of animal sacrifices to the Lord.	1 Samuel 2:12–17, 22–25
	OT	Ahab and Jezebel steal Naboth's vineyard.	1 Kings 21:1–16
	NT	Caiaphas deciding to get Jesus killed as he is perceived to be a dangerous inconvenience.	John 11:45–53
	NT	Herod arresting John the Baptist because John had pointed out Herod's immoral behaviour. Finally Herod had him killed.	Matthew 14:3–12
	NT	Pontius Pilate agreeing to have Jesus crucified, despite not finding him guilty of any crime, in order to avoid a riot in Jerusalem which would have been organised by the Temple priests.	Matthew 27:11–26
	HP	Professor Dolores Umbridge punishing Harry for claiming that Voldemort had returned by giving him lines to write which cut into his skin leaving permanent scarring.	OP Ch.13

	HP	Harry being accused and taken to Court by Cornelius Fudge for misuse of magic when his Ministry had set Dementors on him, which they denied.	OP Ch.8
	HP	Bartemius Crouch Sr. forcing his house-elf Winky to protect his murderous son Barty, who had escaped from Azkaban prison with his help, during the Quidditch World Cup.	GF Ch.8&9
Do your parents, and your upbring-ing have to determine the person you become?	OT	Gideon, who was the youngest member of the least important tribe, is called by God to lead the Israelites against their enemies.	Judges 6:11–7:24
	NT	Paul's impeccable Jewish pedigree causing him initially to persecute Christians, but he becomes con-vinced of Jesus' Messiahship.	Acts 9:1-22 and Philippians 3:4–11
	NT	Mary Magdalene had been delivered of seven demons and was chosen by the risen Jesus to be the apostle to the apostles.	Mark 16: 9–11 and John 20:11–18
	HP	Compare and contrast the upbring-ings of Harry Potter, Severus Snape and Lord Voldemort, and how they turned out as adults.	Various
Things worth giving up or even dying for	OT	Abraham being prepared to sacrifice his son Isaac in obedience to God.	Genesis 22:1–19
	NT	Jesus said that there is no greater love than that of a person laying down their life for their friends.	John 15:12–17

	NT	Jesus dying for us, in order to reconcile us to God.	Philippians 2:3–11
	HP	Harry repeatedly risking death.	
	HP	Ron sacrificing himself as a chess piece while playing wizards, chess so Harry can continue with his quest.	PS Ch.16
	HP	Final Battle of Hogwarts.	DH Chs. 31, 34
	HP	Sirius' telling Peter Pettigrew that he should have been prepared to die rather than betray Harry's parents to Lord Voldemort.	PA Ch.19
Bereavement	OT	Bathsheba grieving for her husband Uriah, murdered by King David, and then David grieving for his and her son who died.	2 Samuel 11:26 and 2 Samuel 12:13–23
	OT	David grieving over the death of his son Absalom, even though Absalom had rebelled against him.	2 Samuel 18:24–19:8
	NT	Jesus weeping over the death of Lazarus with his family.	John 11: 1–37
	NT	Mary Magdalene at Jesus' tomb.	John 20: 1–18
	HP	Harry grieving for the parents he never knew when seeing their reflections in the Mirror of Erised.	PS Ch.12
	HP	Cho Chang grieving for Cedric Diggory.	OP Ch.21
	HP	Harry grieving for Sirius and Dobby.	OP Ch.37, DH Ch.24
The afterlife	OT/NT	The rule of 'One like the Son of Man'.	Daniel 7:13 14 and Revelation 7:9–end

	NT	Jesus' conversation with Martha.	John 11:17-27
	NT	Jesus' promise to the thief on the Cross.	Luke 23:39–43
	HP	Voices are heard through the veil hanging from the arch separating the living from the dead in the Department of Mysteries.	OP Ch. 34
	HP	Harry meets the dead Dumbledore in a vision.	DH Ch.35
	HP	Harry summons visions of his parents, Sirius and Lupin from the Resurrection Stone.	DH Ch.34